the
REFERABLE
SPEAKER

Your guide to
building a sustainable
speaking career—
no fame required

the

REFERABLE
SPEAKER

michael port | andrew davis

**PAGE
TWO**

ISBN 978-1-77458-118-6 (paperback)
ISBN 978-1-77458-119-3 (ebook)

Page Two
pagetwo.com

Edited by Amanda Lewis
Copyedited by Rachel Ironstone
Proofread by Alison Strobel
Cover and interior design by Peter Cocking
Illustrations by Sienna Roman

TheReferableSpeaker.com

To all the speakers who were gracious enough to
share their wisdom with us so we can share it with you.

Contents

Introduction
How We'll Do Transformational Work *1*

PART ONE **THE REFERABLE SPEAKER** *7*

1 **You Don't Get Keynotes, You Earn Them** *11*
Overnight success · Cocktail hour epiphany
The speech is the cake

2 **Your Side of the Business** *21*
Stageside leads · Compounding gigs · The referral tree

3 **Their Side of the Business** *35*
Actors, Athletes, and Astronauts
A-List Alternates · Industry Icons · Surprise and Delight

BREAK **BEHIND THE CURTAIN** *49*
The $18/hour speaker · Audiences walking out
Wanting to quit

PART TWO **THE F+E+E FACTORS** *67*

4 **The Fame Factor** *73*
Worldly • Domain • Fractal

5 **The Entertainment Factor** *93*
Signature bits • Reliable delivery
Transformational experiences

6 **The Expertise Factor** *153*
The Audience Hierarchy of Needs • The positioning problem
The Perception Pyramid • Contextual models

7 **Out of Expertville and into Visionary Town** *189*
Expert sessions versus visionary keynotes
The One Question

8 **You Have What It Takes** *201*
Working backwards • Create history

Conclusion Stay Humble *205*

Acknowledgments *209*

Introduction
How We'll Do
Transformational Work

"FEED THE people who are hungry," says Shep Gordon. Shep Gordon says this a lot. You may not know who Shep Gordon is, but you certainly know some of his clients. Perhaps you've heard of Bette Davis, Raquel Welch, Emeril Lagasse, Salvador Dalí, or Sylvester Stallone? He's also worked with Janis Joplin, Blondie, and Jimi Hendrix.

Shep Gordon is one of Hollywood's most prolific talent managers. He oversees the day-to-day business affairs of his clients and provides advice and counsel to them on professional matters. Shep helps them realize long-term plans and rationalize personal decisions that may affect their careers. Shep is a shepherd: he protects, guides, watches, and tends to his flock of talent. And he does all of this without ever asking his clients to sign a contract.

That's right. Shep Gordon does business over a simple handshake.

We have Shep Gordon to thank for cultivating Alice Cooper's outrageous image. It was Shep Gordon who saved Teddy Pendergrass from exploitation and resurrected Groucho Marx from financial anarchy (pro bono). In an industry known for its ruthless business deals, ego-driven personalities, and backstabbing, Shep is an anomaly.

Shep believes in making fair deals. He believes in kindness and generosity above all. He shares his insight, wisdom, industry contacts, and knowledge freely. For most of his clients, Shep is not just a manager, he's a friend. When Mike Myers hit a personal and professional rough patch, Shep and Mike became housemates. Not just for a couple of days, but for months.

We wish everyone had access to their very own Shep Gordon. That's why we're writing this book. We want to be your Shep Gordon as you build your professional speaking career.

Professional speaking can be lonely. There are the long flights and the tables for one. There are the endless hotel rooms and the steady stream of cocktail hours with unfamiliar faces. And, on a virtual keynote, you won't even get to experience the electric energy of a live audience. Sure, there's an internet's worth of advice on how to book more gigs, create a TEDx Talk, market yourself as a speaker, and create a great slide deck, but we've noticed it's missing the Shep Gordon kind of business advice: the kind that tells you how to show up, how to deliver, and how to book your next gig.

When Shep says, "Feed the people who are hungry," he means give the audience what they want and share your bounty.

Are you hungry?

We sure hope so.

But before we agree to work together, we should be clear about a few things.

We expect that the work we do with you throughout this book will be transformational. That means it might also be provocative. It'll excite you, but it might also challenge you.

You may discover that you need to change the way you think about yourself as a professional speaker.

You may discover that you need to change the way you approach the business of professional speaking.

You may discover that you need to change the way you develop and rehearse your speeches.

And you may be surprised by how much you *want* to make these changes.

So, before we dive in, let's set some rules that will keep you safe and help you stay focused on what you are here to achieve: personal and professional success as a speaker.

Rule 1: We're here to do deep, transformational work

This book is not a series of steps and checklists you must follow in order to achieve speaking success. The book on its own isn't a path to success. You can't just paint by numbers and be a successful creative artist.

Instead, this is a guidebook for something bigger than just securing more gigs. It's a book about doing deep work. It's a book about self-reflection through honest and accurate self-assessment. It's a book about what it takes to be a humble servant in service of an audience.

Rule 2: The only person you should try to be better than is the person you are today

The journey to becoming a successful speaker isn't the same for everyone. It's a quest: a long, arduous journey full of pitfalls and plot twists. It's a seemingly simple business, yet hidden nuances and surprising subtleties arise along the way.

Your quest will be different from ours, and we know that. The size of the stages you speak on, the number of virtual gigs you do, and the fees you charge may be bigger or smaller than ours. The audiences you inspire will be different from ours. That's why we've gathered dozens of other speakers' stories and shared them in this book.

But, please, don't begrudge other speakers' success stories. It's poison to think like that, and it'll destroy you. You're making art, and there is no yardstick that measures art. Be happy for other people's success, and they'll pave the way for you too. In fact, just be happy and you'll work more.

Rule 3: Most people are doing their best, even when you think they're not

We truly believe that our colleagues are doing their best. If a speaker knew how to do a better job, don't you think they would? So rather than criticizing other speakers for not living up to your standards (and, let's be real, you might not be living up to them either), do your best to admire those who take the stage in hopes of making the world a better place—even if you don't love everything they do. Anyone can tear something down. Building something better today than you could yesterday takes courage and character.

Take to heart this advice from Carol Burnett, "Let everybody shine, because that's the best way to look good."

Rule 4: You can't skip Act II

As a storyteller, you know that you can't skip Act II. In fact, Act II is where a masterful storyteller spends most of their time because the lifeblood of a story lives in the conflict in Act II. If you skip the conflict, the resolution has little meaning.

The same holds true for your life and work. We're asking you to do the hard work of becoming a referable speaker because it's the only sure way to achieve your goals. Your success as a speaker is entirely in your hands and relies on embracing the emotional challenges that accompany a quest of epic proportions. Taking a helicopter to the top of a mountain is easy but, ultimately, the thrill fades. You'll have the pictures to say you were there, but if you actually do the difficult work of climbing the mountain, you will forge your character and inform your life for years to come.

Rule 5: Toughen up, buttercup

By the end of this book, you may feel overwhelmed. You may suddenly find yourself with a long list of things you could or should do to improve your speech, transform your approach, or even change your fee structure.

You may need to toughen up.

We hope this book changes the way you look at the speaking business. If you're new to this business, you'll be happy to know that this book will set you up for success. We'll break down exactly how organizers find and book their speakers. We'll show you how to build a referable speech, and we'll give you the simple question that the most sought-after speakers in the world have answered for themselves.

The more experience you have as a speaker, the more challenging the book may be. So, don't just read this book with an eye to pick up a few tips or tricks. Tips and tricks are for amateurs looking for a shortcut. Professionals are on a quest to transform their speaking business, one speech and one audience at a time.

Now, let's do the work.

— *part one* —

THE REFERABLE SPEAKER

B EING A referable speaker is the best way to explain the meteoric rise of a previously unknown keynoter, or the longevity of the speaker who does a hundred keynotes a year, every year, for a decade.

It's the simple reason one free webinar can result in ten paid virtual keynotes.

It's the only way to understand how a speaker can transform a keynote speech into a bestseller, or why some speakers find themselves stuck in small breakout rooms at big events while they wish they were on the mainstage.

It's the reason some speakers command fees five times what others in the same area of expertise receive, while still others plateau at the same rate for years.

To be a *referable speaker*—using the gigs you get to get the gigs you want—requires that you craft a referable speech, a keynote-caliber session that reliably delivers new inquiries to speak at other events.

Do this, and you, too, will become a referable speaker.

(1)

You Don't Get Keynotes, You Earn Them

ANDREW PICKERING and Pete Garland can pinpoint the exact day they became referable speakers.

Until that moment, Andrew and Pete, a speaking duo from Newcastle upon Tyne, UK, had spent five years speaking for free all over Europe. Yes, *free*. Andrew and Pete had been delivering breakout sessions for the occasional travel stipend and a modest honorarium, but often they spoke for free.

Their forty-five-minute sessions were uniquely fun, fast-paced, and packed with practical advice the audience could take home and take action on the next day. Their post-event survey rankings continually scored high, and organizers' feedback was positive. At cocktail hour, attendees would crowd around the two to ask questions and learn more.

Andrew and Pete felt they were good speakers, but they wanted more. They wanted to keynote the marketing industry's biggest events, and they dreamed of speaking in front of thousands instead of hundreds.

Andrew and Pete were feeling discouraged. They'd even spent their own money to deliver a breakout session at a marketing conference in Cleveland, Ohio. The event organizer was thrilled because audience feedback was overwhelmingly positive. But those keynote invitations they'd hoped would roll in hadn't materialized. They knew that if they were ever going to land the coveted keynote stages, their approach would have to change, dramatically.

When they were invited to present in front of three hundred entrepreneurs in London in the fall of 2018, they decided this speech had to be different. So, every single day, sometimes for four or five hours, they worked on their speech. Not the old tips and tricks speech based on best practices, but a brand-new big idea speech, a transformational visionary idea that would change the way their audiences saw the world of marketing.

Sometimes, they'd write and rehearse the same five minutes over and over until they couldn't tell if it was terrific or terrible. Other days, they'd share the big idea in their new talk with a few peers for their feedback.

On weekends and late into the night, Andrew and Pete would refine their speech. Some days they'd search for new stories to add. Others, they'd share one of their "tweetable moments" on Instagram to see if it resonated with their audience. They'd kill what didn't work and elevate what did. They were ruthless.

Then, on November 4, 2018, they debuted their new keynote speech, "The 90:10 Rule," at the Youpreneur Summit in London, and the audience loved it. Before they'd even walked off the stage, National Speakers Association Hall of Famer and emcee Jay Baer texted the event organizers at Social Media Marketing World, one of the largest social media conferences in the world: "At the Youpreneur Summit watching [Andrew Pickering and Pete Garland's] new talk. Incredible. Think about them for your keynote in 2019. It's that good."

Andrew Pickering and Pete Garland became referable speakers.

One event, one speech, changed everything. Those hundreds of other free gigs hadn't generated even one keynote opportunity. All those breakout sessions packed with actionable takeaways generated tons of buzz, great session feedback, and a bunch of new YouTube subscribers, but no one had ever before suggested they keynote an event in front of thousands.

What exactly did these two young guys do in their new speech to become the closing keynote speakers at one of their industry's biggest events?

Cocktail hour epiphany

There was a time, not very long ago, when Ann Handley customized every single presentation to every audience. She'd been told that meetings planners, and the audiences they serve, want customized presentations.

As a writer first and a speaker second, Ann knows that the secret to connecting with any audience is to get to know them. Ann's also instinctively curious. She loves to spend an afternoon chasing links to find a funny, off-beat, relevant, and compelling story.

Sometimes, Ann starts by reading her audience's trade publications and signing up for a handful of corporate newsletters. She'll dissect their confirmation emails and pore over their "About Us" pages. Other times, Ann will consume two years' worth of corporate blog posts, watch hours of YouTube videos, or scour the insiders' social media feeds looking for a nugget of a good story.

As a result of her digging, Ann unearths the most delightful tales to incorporate into each speech, relevant anecdotes she knows the audience will appreciate. No wonder Ann is one of the most sought-after speakers in the marketing world. She's funny, irreverent, and unbelievably smart. Audiences and event organizers love Ann. We do too.

But in 2015, something strange happened.

Ann was booked to do a fifteen-city speaking tour, and her client wanted the same speech in each city.

"One speech, fifteen cities, the same audience?" Ann thought. "That sounds great! That's way easier than customizing all fifteen speeches."

In the first city, the speech went well. The audience seemed to enjoy it. But Ann thought it could be better, so she tweaked a few things.

By the fourth city, Ann had tightened up the stories, and her one-liners got punchier.

By the sixth city, Ann had refined her slides and even noticed more smartphones going up to take pictures when she hit the salient lessons in each story.

At a cocktail hour after her keynote at the seventh stop on tour, Ann remembers the exact moment she became a referable speaker.

"A group of people from a Fortune 500 tech company's partner program came up to me at cocktail hour and said something I'd never heard anyone say before. 'Can you give that exact same speech to our partners?'"

Ann had fielded hundreds of invitations to speak at events, but this request was different. She couldn't remember a time when someone had asked for the exact same speech.

The folks from the Fortune 500 company didn't want a customized version of the speech she'd delivered earlier in the day; they wanted *that exact same speech.*

A year later, Ann gave that speech at the Global Partner Summit for double her original fee. Except, only Ann knows it wasn't the exact same speech. It was even better. Sure, all the stories were the same, even the main lessons she delivered were the same, but the truth is, she's never stopped refining that speech.

Seasoned speakers will tell you that Ann's success is a direct result of the reps she's put in on stages big and small.

Meeting planners will point to Ann's unique storytelling style, gracious personality, and her charismatic stage presence as the reason she's so well loved.

Marketers will tell you it's Ann's sizable online following that's led to her higher fees and perpetual speaking demand.

Publishers will point to Ann's *Wall Street Journal* bestseller, *Everybody Writes,* as the reason people entrust her with their audiences.

While all of these things are true, they don't explain why Ann's speaking business took off like a rocket ship after that seventh city on a fifteen-city tour. After all, that might have been the first time Ann was asked for the exact same speech, but it's far from the last.

The speech is the cake

Andrew Pickering and Pete Garland's "overnight" success and Ann Handley's cocktail hour epiphany are textbook examples of a referable speaker in action.

First, they demonstrate the power of a single referral. Andrew Pickering and Pete Garland's speech wasn't even over when Jay Baer sent the text message that would help them secure the keynote at the world's largest social media conference.

No one asked Ann for her credentials. They didn't ask her to justify her fee when they approached her at cocktail hour asking for the exact same speech.

Referrals from people who've already seen you speak close faster, at higher fees, with fewer objections than opportunities from any other source.

Additionally, in both cases the transformation from speaker to referable speaker happened only when they refined the same speech over and over and over.

In 2015, Ann's client gave her permission to deliver the very same keynote in every city, but Ann's deep-seated desire to continuously tweak and refine that one speech turned it into something other people wanted. In Andrew and Pete's case, their unwavering focus on creating a new speech for one event and investing the time and energy into perfecting it propelled them into a new tier of speaker. Both Ann and Andrew and Pete have seen a precipitous drop in their requests for "customized" presentations ever since they became referable speakers.

Finally, in both cases, their speaking success has had little (if anything) to do with their ability to market themselves as speakers or to build their personal brands. Ann's bestselling books, her personable online presence, and her executive-level leadership experience all exist at the periphery of the speech she delivered at the seventh city on a fifteen-city tour. All of her accolades and accomplishments are icing on the cake.

The speech is the cake.

Andrew Pickering and Pete Garland are no different: their successful membership business, their noteworthy YouTube channel, the two books they've published, even their ranking as two of the top marketers in the world didn't change the market's perception that Andrew and Pete are great breakout session speakers. Only a new kind of speech did that.

These three characteristics—rapid referrals, a continuously refined speech, and a focus on the experience instead of their personal branding or marketing—define how a speaker moves from breakout sessions to the keynote stage overnight, or why some speakers can give the same speech for over a decade and still increase their fees.

Of these three characteristics, the first, rapid referrals, is the most important. It's the concept that makes sense of the second two and gives us the greatest insight into evaluating the success of any single speech or gig.

Rapid referrals from audience members who've seen you speak close faster, at higher fees, more often than any other referral or lead source. Why? Because they've seen what you can do and want exactly that speech for their event and their audience.

Measuring your speaking success by the number of referrals you receive bucks much of the speaking advice you might hear: You need to market yourself better. You need a slick website with arresting imagery. You need a sizzle reel that knocks the socks off the event organizers visiting your website. You need a speaker one-sheet showcasing your significant list of accomplishments. You need to gather a mailing list and do some outbound marketing. You're going to need to buy some keywords and invest in a little advertising. You need to write a bestselling book and secure a speakers' bureau to represent you. Market yourself better if you want to win more gigs, more often, at higher fees.

That advice isn't wrong: all of those things might help you get *one* gig.

None of it will guarantee you get the *next* gig.

The only thing that will help you turn one gig into one dozen is a speech that generates new opportunities to speak at other events online or in person.

Instead of focusing on getting one gig at a time, you should focus on turning the gigs you get into just a few more.

Those gigs will get you a few more gigs, and, before you know it, you're looking at a full calendar of high-level, high-paying keynote speeches.

The product isn't you. It's your speech.

Consistently deliver a finely crafted keynote and a seamless experience for the meeting planner. Build a stellar rapport when you're not onstage or online, and you'll find yourself generating new speaking opportunities every single time you step off the stage or turn off your camera.

You don't *get* keynotes. You *earn* them.

This elegantly simple but ultimately powerful idea will transform the way you look at the speaking business—and it *is* a business.

CALLBACKS

- Referrals from people who've already seen you speak close faster, at higher fees, with fewer objections than opportunities from any other source.

- Instead of focusing on getting one gig at a time, you should focus on turning the gigs you get into just a few more.

- The product isn't you. It's your speech. This elegantly simple but ultimately powerful idea will transform the way you look at the speaking business—and it *is* a business.

(2)

Your Side of the Business

J UST LIKE any business, the speaking business is governed by the simple laws of supply and demand.

Increase demand, and you can increase your fees.

Craft a referable speech, and every single time you deliver a speech you will increase demand.

Increase demand enough, and find yourself securing so many speaking inquiries it exceeds the supply of dates you're available, which means you can increase your fee even more.

As you become even better known, maybe you ultimately write that bestselling book or find yourself featured in the *New York Times*, or your podcast hits number one, or your YouTube series takes off, and suddenly you're even more valuable. So you increase your fee again.

Before you're famous, meeting planners buy your speech, your ideas, and then you—in that order. When you become famous, the inverse is true: event organizers buy you, your ideas, and then your speech.

This simple truth is why the conventional but *misguided* advice in the speaking business is to first market yourself, your experience, and your expertise. The industry's best-known speakers market themselves.

The difference between them and you is: they've earned it. They've already crafted referable speeches.

Take a moment to consider the hours each week you might spend building your personal brand and marketing yourself as a speaker. Maybe you spend a few hours prospecting for new events and a couple more hours filling out those requests for speakers forms online. Perhaps you spend some time writing new website copy and crafting the perfect posts for Instagram, Twitter, and LinkedIn. You might commit to writing a new blog post every week to position yourself as a thought-leader. You may spend hours launching your new podcast or YouTube channel. Or maybe you're convinced the reason you're not winning those keynote slots is because you're not yet an author, so you're investing hours working on the book that will surely catapult you into the limelight.

Add it all up and you could be spending ten, twelve, fifteen, or twenty hours a week marketing yourself as a speaker and thought-leader.

Becoming a referable speaker is a trade-off. Instead of spending all those hours marketing yourself and building your personal brand, you're going to reinvest much of that time in your speech. Because, remember, until you're famous, your speech is your product.

Many of the world's most-booked speakers cannot identify exactly what they did to reach the pinnacle of speaker success. Ask them for advice on building a career like theirs, and you'll often hear things like, "You've just got to put in the reps," or "After years and years of chamber of commerce dinners and speeches at local Elks clubs, you, too, can build a successful speaking business." "You've got to get out there and speak," they say.

The truth is, it was all those reps, for those who survived, that helped craft a referable speech. Those successful speakers aren't exactly sure how they did it because they tweaked so many things, so many times, at so many events that they can't point to the few things that make their sessions so referable. But we can.

Most event organizers work on booking their in-person keynote speakers about six months before the event. For virtual events, it's about ninety days prior. We know this because we've been tracking inquiry data for the better part of the last decade, and the average in-person inquiry arrives five and a half months before the event date. Which means if you deliver a referable speech today and someone in that audience decides to invite you to keynote their event, it's highly likely that it's going to be for a date about six months out.

If you're not receiving new inquiries from your current speeches, you can assume that in six months you're going to find yourself wondering where all the gigs have gone.

The secret to generating more business is to start turning your speech into a referable speech—today. How do you know your speech is on the right track? How do you know when you've become a referable speaker?

It all boils down to a few speaking business fundamentals.

Stageside leads

For Andrew and Pete, the notion of delivering a keynote at the world's largest social media marketing conference had seemed far-fetched. Yet, there they were, six months later, delivering the very same speech to four thousand people in San Diego, and the audience loved it.

The instant Jay Baer texted the organizers of Social Media Marketing World was the instant Andrew Pickering and Pete Garland received their very first *stageside lead*—the first speaking business fundamental. And it worked.

By the time Andrew and Pete landed back in the UK after Social Media Marketing World, they started fielding inquiries to keynote events as far away as South America and Australia. They had finally cracked the code. In less than six months, they'd crafted a referable speech that consistently generated stageside leads.

They're called stageside leads because, very often, they happen as soon as we walk off the stage (or turn off our virtual studio ring lights). Someone from the audience comes up to us right after we finish speaking and says something like, "Wow! That was fantastic. We'd love to have you speak at our user conference on March 25th in Provo, Utah. Are you available, and what's your fee?"

Not all of your referrals will occur stageside, but the fastest converting ones will. We call these *hot stageside leads*. Sometimes they'll fill out a form on your website while you're in the middle of a virtual event or while you're eating lunch with attendees. Sometimes a referral will arrive via email two days after you speak. That's a *warm stageside lead*. Other times, a *cold stageside lead* will roll in a few months after the event. The closer the referral arrives to the date they saw you speak, the warmer the lead.

No matter when they arrive, leads from people who've seen you speak are a clear sign you are delivering a referable speech. But the speech isn't finished when you sporadically get a few stageside leads. In fact, the speech is never finished. It can always be better.

As you're first honing your speech, those leads drip in, one here and one there, inconsistent and spotty like Andrew and Pete's first leads. When you start nailing every session, that drip turns into a consistent stream of new leads each and every time you step offstage.

So, if you're delivering a free fifteen-minute lunch-and-learn at the local coworking space, or you just finished a free webinar, and even one attendee says, "That was so interesting! I'm on the board of the local Chamber of Commerce and we have an annual dinner coming up. Would you be available to expand that presentation and give the annual keynote?" then you've done it. You've received your first stageside lead.

Stageside leads are a clear indicator of future success. It takes the subjectivity out of the speaking business and puts your success squarely in your control. Nothing is a better gauge of your future speaking success than the volume, quality, and consistent flow of stageside leads.

If you're not yet generating stageside leads for keynotes, you're not yet delivering a referable speech.

The power of compounding gigs

In 2010, Andrew Davis, this book's coauthor, spoke at a conference for $5,000.

That one event generated three stageside leads, for which he increased his fee to $10,000.

Those next three events each generated three stageside leads for a total of nine new leads. So, again, he raised his fee.

Those nine events turned into twenty-seven more stageside leads, and over and over again he increased his fee.

Within two years, Andrew had increased his fee to $17,000 per event and completed thirty gigs, for a total of $465,000 in revenue. All of this from one gig where he delivered a referable speech that reliably generated stageside leads.

This is the power of compounding gigs, the second speaking business fundamental: the more gigs you do, the more stageside leads you'll earn, and the more gigs you'll book.

In finance, compound interest is a method of calculating interest, where interest earned over time is added to the principal. So, the more money you invest, the more growth you'll see, assuming, of course, the underlying asset is performing well by increasing in value.

The same is true for compounding gigs. If your underlying asset (your speech) is performing well or, we should say, is *performed* well, it will earn interest over time through new leads that you convert into new gigs.

Imagine you reliably generate four stageside leads each time you get onstage.

The first gig generates four leads. Two of those leads are won. Those two gigs generate eight new leads. Half of those are won. Twenty-four months later, one event has turned into a hundred and twenty-four stageside leads and thirty-one gigs. A referable speech inherently increases your demand in the marketplace, and the more in-demand you are the more you can charge for each gig.

The Power of Compounding Gigs

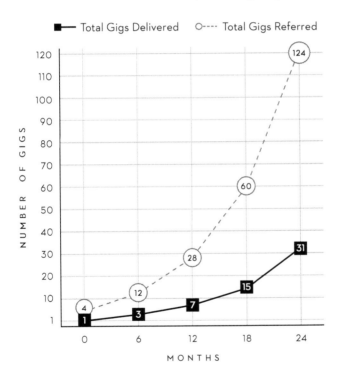

The more your referable speech reliably produces stageside leads, the more predictable your business becomes. The more predictable your business becomes, the more you can increase your fee.

Stageside leads are the key to increasing your fee. Even if you're already booking gigs, in order to increase your fee over time, it helps to quote a fee that's a speaking season ahead. Otherwise, you may find yourself resenting the gigs you do because you are doing them for too little. So, if you spoke at an event today for $2,500 and you receive a stageside lead for six months from now, you would quote the fee you expect six months from now (perhaps $4,000), not the fee you spoke for at this event.

It's important to remember that increasing your fee happens over time and is predicated on your ability to generate stageside leads. If you're not receiving more than one stageside lead from every event, you shouldn't increase your fee—yet.

Compounding gigs leverage the most under-appreciated aspect of the speaking business: the referral tree.

The referral tree

Dr. Elliot Eisenberg is famous for being a funny economist (oxymoron, right?).

To be frank, Dr. Eisenberg isn't very famous among his peers in the economics world. He hasn't won a Nobel Prize. He hasn't taught economics at the most prestigious universities. He never ran a country's economy, a bank, or even a hedge fund. But, if you're in the home building or mortgage business, chances are you know Dr. Elliot Eisenberg.

Dr. Eisenberg served as the senior economist with the National Association of Home Builders in Washington, D.C., and created the world's first multifamily stock index. In the world of apartment building finance, this is a big deal. Naturally, when he first started speaking in front of audiences, it was in the home building world.

It turns out Dr. Eisenberg has a knack for explaining complicated economic principles, trends, and forecasts in a very accessible way. "I talk about economics without boring you to death," promises his Twitter profile. He's not just interesting, his presentations are entertaining. His boundless energy, well-timed jokes, and simple (yet powerful) economic insights make for a perfectly referable speech. His signature bit includes the very buttoned-up, bow-tie-wearing economist climbing onto an eight-foot round table in the middle of the audience to make a point. It's priceless.

It wasn't long before a credit union executive who'd seen Dr. Eisenberg at a mortgage industry event asked if he'd be willing to speak at an association event for credit unions. Dr. Eisenberg took the gig, and within a year, he'd done seven more credit union events. At another banking industry event, he got a stageside lead inviting him to speak at an energy event. At that energy industry conference, he was invited to speak at the annual Georgia Oilmen's Association event in Amelia Island, Florida.

There, one of the stageside leads asked if Elliot had ever spoken to an audience of jobbers, the professionals who wholesale fuel and sell it directly to the end user, such as for an airline or for home heating oil. Over the next couple of years, Dr. Eisenberg presented at a half-dozen jobber conferences around the country.

In the past decade, Dr. Eisenberg's stageside leads have sprouted into some really interesting branches: kitchen surface manufacturers and contractors, mobile home park owners, appliance manufacturers and retailers, realtors, co-ops, and vinyl siding installers.

Dr. Elliot Eisenberg has grown a healthy referral tree.

A *referral tree* is a map of the gigs that led to other gigs. Dr. Eisenberg's first mortgage industry event led to the credit union branch. The banking event branch led to an energy branch and the oil industry event. The oil industry event branches into the first jobber event, which branches into more jobber events ... and on and on the tree grows.

Every time Dr. Eisenberg is introduced to a new branch, by doing the initial gig in a new industry, he's becoming more famous in very specific areas and, as a result, he's booking more gigs on a specific branch. With each new branch, he's growing his fame in a new area. Dr. Eisenberg has become a big fish in a bunch of small ponds: the jobber pond, the vinyl siding pond, the contractor pond, the credit union pond ...

Sure, maybe Dr. Eisenberg would still love to find himself on the stage delivering a Nobel Prize acceptance speech, or keynoting a session at the World Economic Forum in Davos, both of which might be considered the pinnacle of the economic industry's speaking opportunities. Either one of those two events would turn Dr. Eisenberg into one of the most famous economists in the world.

But the truth is, he needs neither of those to build a profitable, sustainable, ever-growing speaking business. Today,

The Referral Tree

EXAMPLE: DR. ELIOT EISENBERG

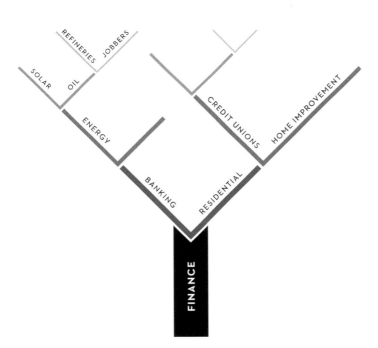

Dr. Eisenberg's referral tree is so healthy he does about a hundred keynote speeches a year.

"I do no marketing," Dr. Eisenberg said in an interview with us. "I just answer a ringing phone."

In 2020, keynote speaker and emcee Jay Baer and his agent, Michelle Joyce, partnered with SpeakInc to find out how meeting planners select their speakers. After surveying 150 meeting organizers, they tallied the responses.

No matter how you slice the data, the top three ways that meeting planners select and find their speakers are:

1 See the speaker elsewhere.
2 Word of mouth from other meeting professionals.
3 Word of mouth from other people in their organization who are not meeting professionals.

That's right. The top three ways meeting planners secure their speakers is *by referral.*

Understanding and leveraging the ways in which your referral network grows is one of the most under-rated and under-appreciated aspects of the speaking business. Those who lean into their referral trees and embrace each new branch take advantage of the power of compounding gigs. Those who meander aimlessly from one gig to another without any idea how they got each gig or the one before it miss an opportunity to shape their career, increase their fees, and secure more gigs.

Mapping your referral tree allows you to rapidly uncover new branches of opportunity. If you're receiving three or four stageside leads from every event you do, your tree will flourish.

These three speaking business fundamentals—stageside leads, compounding gigs, and the referral tree—are the keys to your success.

CALLBACKS

- Measure the quality of your speech not by the post-event surveys or the number of people who tell you it was great, but by the number of stageside leads you garner.

- Leverage the power of compounding gigs to increase your fee and measure your demand in the marketplace.

- Map your referral tree to better understand where and how you get every gig so you can replicate success in new branches.

(3)

Their Side of the Business

————————

S O FAR, this book has been all about *you*, the speaker. But what about your clients: the meeting planners and event organizers?

If they select their speakers because they've seen the speaker elsewhere, or someone else has, what exactly are they looking for when they see a person speak?

How do meeting planners select their keynote speakers? How do they think about programming an entire event? Where do you fit in?

"When I program an event, I'm really looking for three anchor speakers. Speakers I can build the entire event around," says event organizer Carol Walden. "I need one at the beginning, one at the end, and one somewhere in the middle," she adds as we chat on the phone.

Carol is the former senior vice president, event content and design at Winsight, Media & Events division. She's been producing events for more than two decades, programming the largest of the company's fifty events per year, each of which welcomes as few as sixty people to as many as sixty-five thousand people. Carol is a consummate professional who's booked more than a thousand speakers to headline the biggest and most influential conferences around the world.

Carol is the buyer, the gatekeeper, and the ultimate influencer when it comes to those few coveted keynote slots.

So, how does someone like Carol select her keynote speakers? How does she determine how much to pay them? Where does she find them?

Well, she doesn't find them in her email inbox.

"Can I tell you my pet peeve?" Carol volunteers. "It's speakers, or their representatives, who don't do their homework at all. They don't have the slightest idea what we do before they blast me with emails saying how perfect they would be for my audience."

Like thousands of other meeting organizers, Carol produces trade-related events: meetings, shows, and conventions for four specific industries—restaurant, food-service, convenience store, and grocery. Effective meeting organizers have an intimate and deep understanding of the audiences they serve, and Carol's no exception. She knows exactly what her audience wants, why they attend, and how to ensure the event sells out. "Our audience doesn't want anything they can read in one of our magazines or find online. They want a glimpse into new research, new experiences, and unexpected insight they wouldn't get if they didn't attend," she says.

So, if you're one of those speakers sending organizers like Carol an unsolicited email addressing a topic that can easily be found with a quick Google search, she's not interested. Remember, a referable speaker invests time and energy into crafting a transformational speech instead of spending that time on marketing or outbound sales activities.

Let's take a deep dive into how Carol selects the keynote speakers for a few of her annual events, the Restaurant Leadership Conference, MenuDirections, Convenience Retailing University, and Food Service Technology (FSTEC).

FSTEC attracts more than a thousand food service IT industry executives and technology partners. In Carol's world, this is a modest size event with clear budget parameters. In 2020, Carol selected three anchor speakers:

1 Mayim Bialik, the star of CBS's *Big Bang Theory*. (As teenagers in the '80s, we have fond memories of Mayim as the title character from NBC's *Blossom*.) Mayim's not just a tremendous actor, she's also a neuroscientist and the sort of celebrity the self-proclaimed IT "nerds" enjoy.

2 Ken Jennings, the highest-earning American game show contestant of all time, on *Jeopardy!*

3 Yancey Strickler, the cofounder of Kickstarter.

Carol picks her three anchor speakers from four categories. Mayim falls into the premier (and highest paid) category.

Actors, Athletes, and Astronauts

Not every speaker Carol hires in this category is literally an actor, athlete, or astronaut, and "There's not a thing that Mayim Bialik is going to add to the conversation for an IT guy in the restaurant business," says Carol about her decision to invite the TV star to headline the event, but speakers in this category are the type she hires to fill seats. Carol's hired celebrities like Shaquille O'Neal, Dennis Miller, Adam Savage, Madeleine Albright, Magic Johnson, Arianna Huffington, Scott and Mark Kelly, Condoleezza Rice, Barack Obama, and so many more. They are marquee names—former presidents and politicians, authors and activists, innovators and inventors, actors and comedians, talk show hosts, publishers, and news personalities. These people are famous.

Marquee names such as these add three things to the perceived value of the event: instant name recognition, immediate credibility, and guaranteed attendance. Sure, attendees may skip the panel discussion on cyber security, but we bet they won't miss the chance to see a former president of the United States live and in person for forty-five minutes. So Carol might program that panel discussion right before the president arrives (without a break) to guarantee she has a full house.

As Carol candidly shares, those actors, athletes, and astronauts "brighten our ability to attract the audience that we want. Their inclusion in the program is designed to wow, engage, and attract attendees."

Not every event has a mid-six-figure budget for their three anchor speakers. But one thing is clear—the more recognizable the names on the marquee, the more likely the audience is to attend. In fact, even organizers of small, low-profile events consider how famous their keynote presenters are. Sure, the speaker may not fit squarely into the Actors, Athletes, and Astronauts category, but organizers all evaluate a speaker's name recognition when making their selections and apportioning their budgets.

In short, how famous you are factors heavily into whether you're a good fit for a keynote slot and how much the organizer values your presence, aka how much you can charge for your keynote. There's a direct correlation between your level of fame and the demand you generate in the marketplace.

Mayim Bialik commands a fee almost double what Ken Jennings does because she's more famous and as a result she's in higher demand. (Mayim's notoriety as a famous "nerd" adds even more value for Carol's audience.) The same is true for every other speaker in the world. Understanding how fame factors into your success is extremely important. But it's not the only driver of success.

Okay, so you're not an actor, athlete, or astronaut, like Mayim. That's okay. Neither are Ken Jennings or Yancey Strickler. Carol picks them out of the second category of keynote speakers.

A-List Alternates

"If their names aren't immediately recognizable, the next four to six words better damned well be," says Carol. To be candid, neither of us recognized Yancey's name and only one of us recognized Ken's name until we read the next few words that followed their names. Yancey Strickler is the cofounder of Kickstarter and Ken Jennings has won more games (and money) than any other contestant on *Jeopardy!*

Yancey and Ken are perfect examples of A-List Alternates.

Those in the category of A-List Alternates don't have the immediate name recognition of those in the Actors, Athletes, and Astronauts category. Instead, these keynoters have the privilege of a connection to a company that's a household name (think Apple, Tesla, Amazon, Google, or Starbucks). Or they've achieved something noteworthy in their own right. Perhaps they landed a plane in the Hudson River (Chesley "Sully" Sullenberger III), or lost 239 pounds on *The Biggest Loser* (Danny Cahill).

Carol's hired everyone from world record–holding competitive eaters to accomplished mountain climbers. She's hired artists, musicians, CFOs, professors, and authors who draw interest and attention by being attached to their accomplishments or a brand in a way similar to those categorized as Actors, Athletes, and Astronauts—often without the six-figure price tag or powerhouse cachet. But the A-List Alternates are a viable and valuable addition to any meeting organizers' agenda. At a conference with more budget constraints, they might be slotted as the headliner because a speaker from the Actors, Athletes, and Astronauts category is out of reach.

The A-List Alternates category demonstrates how critical a speaker's accomplishments and brand associations are to an event in terms of the value it brings to marketing and selling the event. Some A-List Alternates are granted a higher perceived value simply because they've been hired by a brand most people admire. Others have achieved something truly unique or amazing in their own right.

In our extensive conversations with event organizers and meeting planners, it's clear that the most conscious choices an event team makes about who to hire and how much they'll pay relate specifically to a speaker's accomplishments or brand association.

Maybe you're getting a little worried. You're not famous like Queen Latifah. You don't work for one of the most coveted brands in the world, and you haven't climbed Everest. Yet.

Don't worry. We've got great news for you: There is a place for you on the keynote mainstage. And this book shows you how to get it. What's important, right now, however, is that, although you don't need to be famous to land coveted keynote spots, it's important that you recognize how heavily fame factors into every event organizer's initial perception of your value at their event.

If Carol has the budget for it, she'll pick a keynoter from the Actors, Athletes, and Astronauts category. Then she often selects from among the A-List Alternates. Next, Carol will look to the third category of keynote speakers.

Industry Icons

While you might not know who Richard Allison Jr. or Emily Sheetz are, the audience that Carol is looking to attract does. If you're in the restaurant business, you'll know that Richard Allison Jr. is the CEO of Domino's Pizza, one of the most successful fast-food brands in the world. If you own a bunch of convenience stores, you'll know that Emily Sheetz is the head of strategy for one of the most successful and innovative chains of convenience stores and coffee shops in America.

Here's the catch: "They've got to be relevant, known to the industry, and be a speaker that people can't have access to on a daily basis," Carol says.

Industry Icons are the Actors, Athletes, and Astronauts for a specific niche. In Carol's case, when programming the FSTEC, they're the IT execs from the biggest and brightest brands in the restaurant and foodservice business. They're the people everyone in the industry would love to meet, learn from, and whose perspective on current challenges or industry innovations they want to hear.

Unless you're already an Industry Icon, there's almost no chance your unsolicited email to Carol is going to hit the mark.

Hearing from an Industry Icon is valuable. Not just to meeting planners and event organizers, but to the executives that hire a speaker. One of the biggest questions an organization has for every speaker that arrives from outside their industry is: will they be relevant? They worry about your ability to truly understand the audience's perspective, their challenges, and their opportunities. Industry Icons are an easy answer to this challenge. One would expect that the CEO of Domino's is going to be relevant to a room full of two thousand restaurateurs.

A word of caution.

We know dozens of speakers who have built successful keynote careers while being affiliated with one of those noteworthy brands. Until one day, they decided to move on. Some started a consulting firm or took on a new role working for a partner. Others retired. And still others were poached to work at smaller, lesser-known brands. Unfortunately, as soon as they lost the aura the brand imbued on their speaking success, all those high-profile speaking gigs dried up. No one wants the former chief marketing officer of Marriott if they can get the current chief marketing officer of Marriott, right?

So, if you currently find yourself being booked as an A-List Alternate, make sure you use this time to work on becoming a referable speaker, so that when you move on (and you will), you'll still garner the stageside leads to keep your career humming. Ask yourself (and answer honestly): Are you being invited to speak because you provide a transformational experience each and every time you step on the stage? Or are you being asked to speak because you work for a brand that garners awe and respect?

If you're not currently a famous actor, athlete, or astronaut, an A-list alternate, or an icon of your industry, you can still be chosen to keynote the high-profile conferences and earn fees from $15,000 to $40,000.

In fact, meeting planners are actively searching for this next category of speaker because they reliably deliver transformational experiences and they do it for far less than Arnold Schwarzenegger.

Audiences love getting their picture taken with Arnold, but this next category of speaker changes the way people see the world. This fourth and final category of keynote speaker provides the perfect balance of entertainment and insight. They deliver the speech that everyone talks about at the cocktail party and back at the office around the water cooler and when working on new initiatives.

They deliver a transformational experience.

The Surprise and Delight speaker

"The Surprise and Delight speaker is the one who provides a bright spark of energy, entertainment, and insight that no one expected," Carol explains. "They're dynamic, and the audience can extrapolate valuable information while being completely entertained."

You might just be the next Surprise and Delight keynote speaker that Carol discovers.

In 2016, Carol attended a convenience association event in Chicago, and that's where she saw one of her favorite Surprise and Delight speakers: David Schonthal. "David speaks about innovation, which is so easy to say these days, but he really delivers," says Carol.

Here's how Carol recounts what she saw:

> David tells one of the funniest stories I've ever heard. It's this hilarious tale about conducting innovation research on prescription bottles. He explains how the survey data signaled that consumers have no trouble opening prescription bottle caps. But David wanted to see this for himself. So, he visits an eighty-year-old survey respondent in her home. When he arrives he realizes she's severely arthritic and asks the woman again if she has

trouble opening prescription bottle caps. "No," she says. "I don't have any trouble at all." So David asks her to demonstrate how she opens them with such ease. That's when the woman takes David to the kitchen where she fires up the meat slicer and runs the prescription bottle cap through the blade. It's really, really, funny. The audience eats it up.

After David's session, Carol sought him out, introduced herself, and asked him if he'd be interested in speaking at her Convenience Retailing University event. "Since then, I've booked him numerous times across several events and audiences because he translates so well," says Carol.

Carol is one of David's stageside leads, and all those other events she's hired David to keynote demonstrate the power of compounding gigs.

David Schonthal surprises and delights audiences, and he does it reliably. No unsolicited email would have secured David a gig with Carol. She had to experience him for herself.

A Surprise and Delight speaker must provide value, but one of the things they bring that the A-List Alternates, the Industry Icons, and the Actors, Athletes, and Astronauts often don't is the entertainment factor. They provide the perfect balance of insight and entertainment. They deliver a transformational experience.

Event organizers love to deliver an experience. They dream of surprising and delighting their audience, and their CEO, with an unexpected home run.

You don't need to be an industry icon, row across the Atlantic, get a job at the hot new start-up, or be as famous as Serena Williams to earn the mainstage. All you have to do is craft an experience that surprises and delights people like Carol and the audiences they serve, and the stage is yours.

There's one thing Actors, Athletes, and Astronauts; A-List Alternates; Industry Icons; and Surprise and Delight speakers have in common: they don't send unsolicited sales emails like this one Carol received a few days after our chat:

Carol,

Hope you are well.

I noticed your conference and think your attendee goals this year and my background would be a perfect fit. I realize you might not be the person to talk to about speaking at the conference, but I thought you may be able to point me in the right direction, if not. It's an exciting time in the restaurant and hospitality industry! I hope we can connect!

They don't need to.

Carol's approach to planning her event agendas is not unique; her ability to clearly articulate it is. In the last decade, we've talked to over a thousand event organizers; while they don't all have catchy names for their A-List Alternates or Industry Icons, they all evaluate every single speaker in all four of the above-mentioned categories using three factors.

Demonstrating a mastery of all three factors transforms you from just a speaker to a referable speaker. The combination of these three factors makes you a Surprise and Delight speaker. Understand, evaluate, and improve in all three areas, and you'll garner the stageside leads you need to build a sustainable speaking business. In Part Two, we'll explore those three factors in detail.

CALLBACKS

- You don't need to be an industry icon, row across the Atlantic, get a job at the hot new start-up, or be as famous as Serena Williams to earn the mainstage. All you have to do is craft an experience that surprises and delights event organizers and the audiences they serve, and the stage is yours.

- A Surprise and Delight speaker often brings something that even the A-List Alternates, Industry Icons, and Actors, Athletes, and Astronauts don't: the perfect balance of insight and entertainment. They deliver a transformational experience.

- There's one thing speakers from all four categories have in common: they don't send unsolicited sales emails . . . and neither should you.

BREAK

Behind the Curtain
Learn from Our
Missteps and Miscues

BEFORE WE get there, let's take a moment to describe how we got here.

We've already shared multiple stories of professional speakers who've found success by becoming a referable speaker, and there are many more ahead. Maybe you're feeling intimidated by the idea of becoming a Surprise and Delight speaker. Perhaps your ego's taken a hit with the realization that you're not yet an A-List Alternate or even an Industry Icon. Or maybe the concept of building a referral tree is depressing when you have no booked gigs on the calendar.

We get it. We've been there.

We don't want you to get the impression that when we stepped out onstage for the first time as speakers we understood the value of a stageside lead or the power of compounding gigs. We had no idea how to set our fees, or how organizers selected their keynotes. We both spent an insane amount of time and energy building our speaking websites, writing our books, and marketing our personal brands when we embarked on our quest to become professional speakers. In the process, we did more wrong than we did right.

We've bombed in front of paying audiences, and we've lost gigs because we forgot to call the prospect back after we misplaced the sticky note that was supposed to remind us. We've raised our speaking fee too high, too fast, and lost gigs as a result. We've found ourselves on the back end of a twelve-hour flight resenting the gig that secured us because they promised us the audience would be high quality and it wasn't. We've gone live in high-stakes virtual events and watched the technology we chose melt down. We've both had to say no to a full-fee gig because we decided to say yes to speak for free in an exotic destination. We've made mistakes (more than we'd like to admit), and we've tried to learn from each and every one.

This book is the culmination of thousands of little failures, hundreds of hours of trial and error, decades of highs and lows, the lessons we learned, the research that resulted, and the insight we gained. This is why we've come to share what we've learned with you, and it's why we decided to do this together.

Andrew's quest

I knew 2013 would be a growth year.

I'd just sold my digital marketing agency and published my first book, *Brandscaping: Unleashing the Power of Partnerships.* I'd set up a speaker website full of arresting imagery, a long bio touting my experience, and what I thought was a pretty slick speaker reel. I reached out to speakers' bureaus in search of representation. Not one bureau ever returned my call. I'd already booked a few speaking gigs on my own and couldn't wait to see my speaking business take off.

I'd set a goal for my speaking business: sixty gigs at $2,500 each for a total of $150,000 for the year.

So, in 2013, I did exactly what event organizers asked: I stacked my forty-five-minute presentations full of actionable insight. I spent days customizing every single presentation. I spent weeks researching niche industries in which I had no experience, pre-interviewed attendees to customize the content, and wrestled the internet to find relevant case studies.

That year, I did almost thirty unique sessions at about $2,500 each for a total of $72,000, less than half of my goal. My amortized wage for 2013 was $35 per hour.

I felt exhausted and deflated.

If you include the expenses I'd laid out for those arresting images, that slick speaker reel, and my fancy website, I made less than $26 an hour.

When you include the travel expenses I'd not charged back to the client, I made less than $18 an hour.

My net revenue for 2013 was $36,720.

"Maybe I don't have what it takes to be a full-time keynote speaker," I said sulkily, as I reviewed the year's numbers. "Maybe I'm an impostor," I felt depressed and disappointed in myself.

I felt lonely.

As I rang in the New Year with less than half a dozen speaking gigs booked for 2014, I resolved to take an objective look at the business of speaking and figure out a formula for success. I started to question all the speaking advice I'd read, watched, and solicited. I threw all of it out. Everything.

I started asking questions about my business, and I answered them with data:

* How many people inquired about having me speak?
* What was their budget?
* When was their event?
* How many attendees?
* Was it a corporate event or an association?
* How much did I quote?
* Did I win or lose the gig?
* What was my speaker rating on the event organizers' post-event evaluation?
* Who were the keynote speakers at the event, and what did they charge?
* How many days elapse between the time an inquiry comes in and the time they sign a contract?
* How often did I reduce my fee?
* What were my busiest weeks of the year?
* What were the slowest?
* How did these event organizers find me?

I used a spreadsheet to track every single datapoint, no matter how small.

I asked every event organizer from 2013 to send me my post-event evaluations, and I pored over every attendee comment. I dismissed nothing as irrelevant, and as much as it pained me, I embraced the negative feedback as an opportunity to improve.

The data revealed a clear picture: if I'd secured the gig as a referral from the right kind of person, event organizers rarely negotiated my fee. They signed a contract faster, paid more, booked further out, and often booked me for more than one event.

I stopped worrying about what was on my website. I stopped researching niche industries and looking for relevant case studies. I stopped pre-interviewing attendees, and I ended the constant customization of my sessions.

I reinvested all that time into crafting a new speech.

I knew that if I was going to hit my 2013 goal in 2014, I'd have to learn to reliably deliver one great speech. I'd need to use the few gigs in the first half of 2014 to generate new leads for the second half of the year. I needed to turn my first gigs into next gigs.

Focusing on the speech felt liberating. I started listening to the questions attendees had about my session with a new ear for improvement. I fixed things that I could tell weren't resonating. I killed things I loved but the audience didn't. I rehearsed and rehearsed and rehearsed before every event. I even took free gigs just to get in front of an audience and to improve.

Instead of analyzing the public personas of speakers I admired, I started analyzing their speeches.

I sat in the back of every keynote I could attend, outlining the speech in real time. I ran my own timer for them so I could note what they talked about when. I created a shorthand for audience reactions: a Cheshire cat grin for audience laughter and a scribbled high-five hand for spontaneous applause. I compiled each outline and compared it to other speeches I'd seen. I listened to the things that other attendees talked about after each keynote. I started identifying holes in my speech, and I worked tirelessly to fix them.

I didn't know it at the time, but I had started crafting an *experience* instead of delivering a speech. Which is exactly why I wanted to write this book with Michael Port. Because there's one thing all that data and business intelligence I've collected since 2013 cannot tell me, but Michael can: what exactly is the difference between a speech and a performance?

Every time I've hit a plateau in my speaking business, Michael has helped me break through. Sometimes, we've spent an entire ten-hour day reworking the same three and a half minutes of a performance until it works. Other times, he's had to push me to give up something I think works in favor of something more challenging (and ultimately more successful).

Those daylong sessions have turned into early morning calls where I've traded my insight about the business of speaking for his advice about a performance I'm working to hone. Every year, Michael and his wife, Amy, see seven hundred public speakers walk through their doors at Heroic Public Speaking. They're constantly helping others refine their message and deliver a performance so those pupils can inspire others around the world.

I've come to learn that Michael and I are friends who share the same simple belief: Craft a speech. Change the world.

All that data I'd gathered (and continue to track) helped me hit and then surpass my revenue goal in 2014. All the early mornings and late nights spent continuously refining my session helped me earn the keynote slot at a number of game-changing events—game-changing not because their logos looked great on my website, but because they'd generated so many new gig inquiries.

In 2015, I quadrupled my fee average, spoke at fifty-nine events, and for every gig I won, I lost two because I charged too much.

The truth is, every single year, I do the same thing I did in 2014: I set new revenue goals. I craft a new performance. I refine that new speech until it generates leads, and I use data to inform which gigs to take and how much to charge.

And I love it.

Don't get me wrong, I have my off days, even off months. Every year, twice a year when the speaking inquiries dry up in June and December, I wonder if the ride is over. I ask myself if anyone will hire me again to speak at their event. And, guess what? The leads show up again. Like clockwork.

You're embarking on your own quest. And this year, yes, this year might be your growth year. But it doesn't need to be frustrating, lonely, depressing, or deflating. That is why we wrote this book.

Michael and I are on the journey with you, and we can't wait to watch you grow.

Embrace every moment and enjoy the journey.

Michael's quest

My quest started in 2003 when I got fed up working for a guy named Chip who would let you know if he didn't like your idea by calling it "stupid." A year after I left my job as the nebulously titled VP of Alternative Programming at Chip's film production, distribution, and exhibition company, it folded. I vowed to find my way toward a meaningful career where people value my contributions.

You'd think I'd already found it. I had an MFA from NYU's Graduate Acting program—arguably one of the top acting schools in the country—and guest-starring roles on hot TV shows like *Sex and the City*, *Law & Order*, and *Third Watch*, plus small roles in films like *The Pelican Brief*, *Down to Earth*, and *The Believer*. After grad school, I gave four years to professional acting, only I didn't find the business of acting interesting, let alone fulfilling.

In between "legit" acting jobs, I did TV commercials for Budweiser, Johnson & Johnson, and Wendy's, and voice-overs for Coors, MTV, Pizza Hut, Braun, and AMC. I was a working actor, and yet, I wasn't satisfied. Spending the day inside a four-by-four-foot recording studio repeating, "Braun. Smart thinking" over and over again began to feel, well, to borrow a word from Chip, stupid. I had gone into acting to study human behavior, not sell pizza, pharmaceuticals, razor blades, and beer.

So I quit acting. I spent the next four years on the business side of the fitness industry and then nine painful months working for Chip.

But then I hung up a shingle as a branding coach for independent business owners. Honestly, I just wanted a job where I could help people, because being a part of someone's transformation is what I find most rewarding.

When I look back at the audacity it took to make this leap, I marvel at my youthful optimism and comfort with risk. In the first year, I struggled to make ends meet while I stumbled around, trying to find my way. At the time, I didn't see it as a quest. But what a quest it's been.

Almost twenty years later, I'm amazed at what I've accomplished despite this inauspicious start. My fourth grade teacher had said I had the worst spelling she'd seen in twenty-five years, and yet I went on to become author of nine books; a few of them even found their way onto the *New York Times*, *Wall Street Journal*, and USA *Today* bestseller lists.

As a keynoter, I've headlined some of the world's largest conferences for the world's most iconic brands on the most storied stages, including Lincoln Center's Avery Fisher (now David Geffen) Hall. In my youth, I thought I'd get on that stage as an actor. Instead, I was the opening keynote speaker for Coldwell Banker, and Tom Selleck followed me. You just never know what the future holds until you quit what isn't working for you.

I "retired" from keynoting when I started coaching professional speakers because I don't want anyone I work with to ever have to worry that they will have to compete with me for a gig. That would be like Roger Federer coaching Rafael Nadal while also still playing Grand Slams. It would just be weird. And, yes, I just compared myself to Roger Federer.

Like all epic quests, my journey has been peppered with accomplishments, but also a plethora of pitfalls and plateaus, mistakes and mirages, and total freaking disasters. Like the time I bombed a high-profile keynote speech in front of more than one thousand people.

There are three types of speakers: those who have bombed, those who haven't bombed but will, and those who have bombed but lie about it. I sit squarely in the first category.

Oh, don't get me wrong. I've given dozens of speeches over the past twenty years that were received with a resounding "meh." When I say *bombed*, I mean people were walking out of the room mid speech. I wish that was the end of it, except the week after that event, the organizers called and asked for a partial refund.

Back then, I frequently gave a keynote speech based on my first book, *Book Yourself Solid*. It was well received and produced stageside leads—it was a referable speech. Then in 2008, I published *The Think Big Manifesto* and it hit the *New York Times* bestseller list, affording me a level of fame I hadn't had before.

So, when the National Association of Productivity & Organizing Professionals (NAPO) asked me to give my first speech based on *The Think Big Manifesto*, I wanted to do something special, something different. And I tried. Sort of.

I worked on my slide deck for two months, but I procrastinated so badly on writing the speech that I had time to do just one run-through before the fateful day. I still remember walking onto the stage, entering from stage left. I even remember the clothes I was wearing: brown boots, jeans, and a pink and white striped button-down shirt (untucked because I had put on some weight).

And then I pretty much read the speech off notes on my computer.

A week later, the meeting planner from NAPO called.

"Hi, Michael—we need to talk."

My heart dropped. I knew why she was calling. I felt humiliated. Just writing about it makes me panicky as I still carry this shame with me.

"Yeah, I'm sorry about that, but the tech wasn't working right and it threw me off," I fibbed.

After that, I turned down every inquiry for a speech based on *The Think Big Manifesto* and went back to giving *Book Yourself Solid* speeches. That's right: the author of a book called *The Think Big Manifesto* gave up because he bombed a speech. (The irony isn't lost on me.)

The worst part was that I knew better. I knew how to rehearse. I knew how to perform. But I didn't do the work. I didn't apply my craft as a former professional actor with an MFA. I thought I could rely on talent and subject matter knowledge—and I was dead wrong. Worse, I gave up. Yet as much as I wanted to bury that speech, it wouldn't die.

Five years later, FILEX, the largest association for fitness professionals in Australia, asked me to hold a date to be the opening keynote at their annual conference for four thousand people. I thought they'd want my speech about *Book Yourself Solid* because it's a perfect keynote for their members. But I wouldn't be so lucky.

They wanted a speech on thinking bigger, and when the word "yes" popped out of my mouth, I immediately wanted to take it back. Maybe I was just in a particularly positive mood because I was on my boat at the time, but it's probably because I wanted their approval.

When I hung up the phone, I began to shake. What did I just do? I scrambled to think of any and every excuse I could use to back out, but instead, I stayed the course.

If I had backed out, that would have probably led my career in a different direction. Sure, I would have kept giving speeches on *Book Yourself Solid*, but I sure wouldn't be where I am today.

Once I signed the contract, I started to plan a six-month production schedule for the speech. During that time, I gave more than five hundred hours to the script development and rehearsal process. It wasn't easy, but it was worth it.

I remember walking onto the stage of the biggest convention center in Australia, again, entering from stage left. I even remember the clothes I was wearing: all black, head to toe.

I also remember that when I finished my speech, the audience leapt to their feet and offered a raucous standing ovation. I can proudly say that I crushed it. I stole the show. Best of all, no one called later to ask for their money back.

It took me five years to get over the failure of that first speech. Five years. I don't want the same for you. But sometimes, coming back from a loss is what we need to carry on.

In fact, coming back from this loss is what raised a career-changing question for me: why don't speakers adequately prepare for high-stakes keynotes?

I knew why *I* didn't: I let my ego get in the way. I thought I could deliver something special without doing anything special to prepare for it.

Is this the same reason so many other speakers think they can create a transformational experience for an audience by winging it?

I realized, however, that even if well-intentioned speakers wanted to put in the work to deliver a referable speech, how would they know how to do it? I had a professional background in performing arts, but most speakers do not.

Which led to another question: why isn't there master's-level training for professional speakers like there is for other creative artists?

So my wife, Amy Port, and I built one. Heroic Public Speaking is an educational institution that offers the most advanced and effective speaker training in the world. Speaker training that is on par with the rigor I experienced in the master's program for acting at NYU and Amy experienced in the master's program at the Yale School of Drama.

We work with CEOs, founders, admirals, astronauts, FBI agents, Olympians, Navy SEALs, politicians (but only the nice ones), mega-bestselling authors, the world's most popular podcasters and YouTubers, and activists who lead movements and advance important causes.

Amy and I, along with our team of speech writers and performance coaches, have developed scripts for and directed many of the most memorable speeches you've seen on the professional speaking circuit.

Twenty years ago, when I started learning about the business side of a speaker's career, I had no clue what I was doing. Most of the time, I was wandering around like a lost little kid looking for approval anywhere I could get it. I did my best to inflate my credentials to look like a big shot. Yet, that's where the lesson was.

I had to stop seeking approval and focus on producing results. As a performer, you don't have complete control over how an audience experiences your work. You do, however, have control over your preparation and performance. If you do everything in your power to deliver on your promises, you can feel good about the work you do.

The first time I gave the "Think Big Revolution" speech, I had an idea of what I wanted to deliver, and I thought I'd be able to bring that idea to life in real time during the speech, but I was wrong. When the stakes were high and the pressure was on, I wasn't able to rise to the occasion.

You won't magically be able to do something you've never actually done before. Instead, you'll fall back on your preparation. If you're not well prepared, it'll become painfully apparent quite quickly. However, if you've done the work, your self-worth will no longer be based on the need for approval. Instead, you will evaluate your work based on the rigor with which you treat your chosen craft and the respect you give your audience.

On second thought, there's another kind of speaker: the well-rehearsed performer who is a master of their craft. You can be that speaker, producing your best work in service of your audience. As you work on your craft, stay focused on how you can be helpful, and you'll quickly become a referable speaker.

Speaking of referable speakers . . . I asked Andrew Davis to collaborate with me on this project because he always delivers on his promises. He's intellectually curious, smart as a whip, cares more about being effective than being right, and makes me laugh—silly little boy giggles, and big hearty belly laughs. Plus, he's just about the only other person I know who will answer my texts at 4:00 a.m., because he's also already up, hammering away at the day's work.

For the past five years, we've joined forces in many ways. I've directed some of his keynote speeches, he's taught the business of public speaking to my advanced students, delivered keynote speeches at Heroic Public Speaking events, and advised my company on our branding efforts. Of the thousands of speakers I've had the honor of supporting over the years, I have yet to meet anyone who works harder at mastering his craft. What's more, he freely shares whatever he discovers along the way. Andrew has made my quest more meaningful and exciting. I hope, as you continue on your journey, you also find opportunities to collaborate with people who help you improve both your work and your character.

Like a transformational speech, a book has the power to change the world and the people in it, including the author. Writing this book for you in collaboration with Andrew has made me a better writer and a more curious thinker.

OUR QUESTS CONTINUE.

We're both far from perfect. We're both still learning. We're constantly questioning what we've done, and looking for ways to make it better. We still hone our craft. We still rehearse and refine, cut and rewrite.

Every speaker's journey is unique, but the themes and emotions are universal. So, when impostor syndrome creeps in, or you bomb onstage, or the tech fails you, or the audience feedback is miserable, remember this: we've been there, and so has every other referable speaker in the world.

Learn from your missteps and miscues. We all have.

THE REFERABLE SPEAKER BUDDY

If it weren't for the honest feedback and support we garnered from our speaker friends, we might never have consistently earned a spot on the keynote stage.

Right now, you don't need dozens of speaker friends. You need one good one. You need a speaker friend who understands your goals, sees your vision, and embraces the change you plan to inspire in others.

You need a friend with whom you can celebrate every stageside lead; a friend you can refer when you're too busy to take every inquiry. You need a referable speaker buddy.

We believe in the speaker buddy system so much that we want you to send a free copy of this book to your referable speaker friend. We imagine you discussing the ideas in this book and challenging each other to build a referable speech. So, buddy up. Right now.

Seriously. Stop reading for thirty seconds and do it. It will change your speaking career forever. All you need is your buddy's email address.

Head to **TheReferableSpeaker.com/myspeakerbuddy**

Write a short personal message, and we'll send them an ebook.

Enjoy the journey. Together.

— *part two* —

THE F+E+E
FACTORS

SOME SPEAKERS earn the keynote slots because they're famous. Others earn the keynote stage because they're experts. Some make it to the keynote stage just because they're entertaining. The referable speaker is the perfect balance of the three factors every event planner considers when they're looking for the perfect keynote speaker: the Fame Factor, the Entertainment Factor, and the Expertise Factor.

These three factors offer a way to evaluate your perceived value for any event. They provide you with direction for where you need to put in the work. They'll help you position yourself better, negotiate smarter, and even understand how the business works more clearly. We call these the F+E+E Factors. The F+E+E Factors illuminate how meeting planners see you.

Fame, entertainment, and expertise are multifaceted. They're nuanced. We're going to break down each factor together.

The three factors—fame, entertainment, and expertise—offer a way for any speaker to make sense of a meeting planner's decision-making process. They provide us with direction for how to go about setting our fees. They help us present our experience and how to best represent our speech.

Before we dissect how each of the three factors affects your journey to becoming a referable speaker, we need to start visualizing each one as a sliding scale.

The Fame Factor is a continuum from *unknown* on one end of the scale to *famous* on the other.

FAME FACTOR

Unknown   Famous

The Entertainment Factor is a continuum from *novice presenter* to *transformational performer*.

ENTERTAINMENT FACTOR

Novice   Transformational
Presenter   Performer

And the Expertise Factor is a continuum from *subject matter expert* to *visionary leader* status.

EXPERTISE FACTOR

Subject Matter   Visionary
Expert   Leader

You can plot anyone, any speaker, even yourself, on the continuum. You can compare speakers using these sliding scales. You can even determine how much you should quote and how much you're worth for a specific event by understanding the nuances for each scale.

The three factors—fame, entertainment, and expertise—will help you chart your path to becoming a referable speaker, but only if you're honest and objective about where you are today on the continuum for each factor.

(4)

The Fame Factor

IT'S APRIL 2006. Myspace is still a big deal and You-Tube is the new kid on the block.

Judson Laipply sits in his Ohio home riffling through his email inbox.

Judson had been building a solid professional speaking career on the college circuit since 1999. His unique blend of inspirational comedy filled his calendar with 130 gigs a year. In the middle of his busy spring speaking season, Judson started to ponder his next move. But what happened next, Judson admits he never could have planned. Not in a million years.

It was a Saturday, and as he sifted through the week's worth of emails he happened on another email from the kids in Connecticut. Almost every day, for a month straight now, a group of kids who'd seen Judson speak had been emailing him with what would seem like a simple request today: could Judson upload a video of his impressive dance performance so they could share it with their friends?

But uploading a video in 2006 was no small task. Judson had to find the right video tape, digitize the video into his computer, edit the video down in iMovie and then find somewhere to host it. After a weekend's worth of work, Judson finally uploaded the video to YouTube, copied and pasted the embedding code into his Myspace profile, and notified those kids in Connecticut. Then, he packed his bags for his Monday morning flight and didn't think twice about it.

At the time, YouTube was a sea of unpredictability. "When you go to this site, you don't really know what to expect," Montana Miller, an assistant professor in the department of popular culture at Bowling Green State University in 2006, told Ryan Smith of the *Toledo Blade* for an article published July 30 that same year. "All you can really predict," Miller continued, "is you're going to see something that surprises you." The average age of a YouTube viewer in April of 2006 was twelve and the number one video on the platform was someone singing the Pokémon theme song.

By today's video production standards, Judson's "Evolution of Dance" YouTube video isn't the highest quality. It's got a charming high school talent show quality about it. Over six minutes, Judson seamlessly moves through forty-four years of popular dance moves. There's Elvis's swiveling hips, the twist, the YMCA, moves from *Grease* and *Saturday Night Fever*. He walks like an Egyptian, moonwalks like Michael Jackson, does the worm, and even busts out the chicken dance. And that's only a few of the moves in the first two minutes. It's a dance video mixtape. It's fun, nostalgic, hilarious, quite impressive, and very well executed. And the talent show crowd is eating it up, clapping along, and having a blast. If you've danced at a party in the last five decades, your dance moves are in Judson's video.

A month later, Judson flew out to San Francisco. He'd been booked to speak at a Kiwanis leadership camp. He checked into the Four Points Sheraton, unpacked his laptop, fired it up, and opened his email. "Someone has liked your video," read the subject line of one email. "Someone has commented on your video," said the next email. There were thirty emails just like this. Judson clicked the link to read the comments and immediately noticed something.

"Holy cow!" he said out loud. "My video has thirty thousand views!" Judson was shocked but hopeful. He thought, "I might get a gig out of this."

The next morning, Judson rented a car and drove the two hours to the Kiwanis camp. The gig went great, and as he headed back into cell phone service range, he flipped open his StarTAC phone to check his email.

Ding. Ding. Ding. Ding. Fifty more email notifications from YouTube flooded his inbox. *Ding. Ding. Ding. Ding.* His voicemail blew up. The first message was from his brother. "Hey Judson, I'm on this email list from a tech guru with a million other subscribers. Did you know that your dance video is featured in his newsletter?"

The next voicemail is from his aunt. "Judson, I get this weekly email newsletter and guess what? Your dance video is in there. It's fantastic!" she says.

In 2006, there was no way to check YouTube on your phone, so Judson called his sister in a panic. She hopped online to check how many views his video has racked up. "Five hundred thousand!" she said. "I'm sorry, I think you're cutting out," Judson responded. "Five hundred thousand views!" Judson's nephew screamed in the background.

In just forty-eight hours, Judson's video had gone viral. It had had been viewed another 470,000 times while Judson was out of cell phone service. Judson's speaking business would never be the same.

On May 19, 2006, just six weeks after uploading his video to YouTube, Judson's "Evolution of Dance" video had been viewed 10,600,000 times and secured its position as the most watched video on YouTube, a position Judson would hold for 652 days straight.

"The phone calls and emails didn't stop," Judson says in a phone chat with us. "It was chaos. I received marriage proposals, and solicitations from Hollywood agents. I got calls from lonely people who said my video made their day and requests for sitcom scripts. And I got tons of gig requests," he says. And then he got a call from YouTube: "Judson, we've been contacted by the *Today Show* on NBC, and they love your video. They want to get in touch with you, and we've never done this before, so we wanted to ask if it's okay if we give them your contact information?"

On June 5, 2006, just sixty-one days after Judson uploaded his video for some tenacious kids in Connecticut, he stood ready to perform a three-minute excerpt of the "Evolution of Dance" live on NBC in New York City.

"It is the video that's taken the internet by storm! In just over a month, Judson's performance has been viewed by— get this—twenty million people!" the host exclaimed as she introduced Judson to the audience of the world's most popular daytime TV program.

Judson performed an abbreviated version of his viral video dance, and the crowd ate it up.

"The internet creates overnight sensations... you're clearly famous now... what are you going to do with this newfound fame?" asked the *Today Show* host.

"I'm going to continue to do exactly what I was doing before: working as a speaker and comedian and hoping to reach as many people as possible. So, if I can take this and use it to reach a larger number of people then I think it's a good thing," he responded.

Over the next few months, Judson would dance at the NBA Finals. He'd be shuttled from a speaking gig to a dance at a wedding reception on a private jet. But more importantly, Judson immediately found himself doing gigs for brands like Sony, GE, AOL, and Wells-Fargo. As a result, Judson more than doubled his fee. Overnight, Judson had broken out of the college speaking market and into the world of corporate clients.

Judson was famous, and his skyrocketing fame had increased demand for his speech.

"Fame is a funny thing. I'd always wanted to be famous," Judson admits. "But not for fame's sake. I wanted to be famous because I knew it would make marketing my speaking business so much easier."

Today, Judson holds a place in internet history as the world's first YouTube celebrity and the creator of the first viral video. His video is still racking up the views (over 300 million as we write). Judson's in an exclusive club of only eighteen videos to hold the coveted spot of "most viewed video on YouTube." That list includes artists like Justin Bieber and Lady Gaga, and songs like "Gangnam Style" and "Despacito."

Judson's right. Fame *is* a funny thing. Loosely defined, fame is the state of being known or talked about by many people. How many is "many"? It depends.

Fame is a continuum—a sliding scale—from unknown to famous.

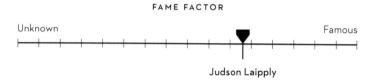

FAME FACTOR

Unknown   Famous

Judson Laipply

Fame is relative and subjective. It's not like you have it or you don't. Which is to say that one's level of fame must be considered in proportion to someone else. If you were a teenager in the 1980s, you might think David Byrne, the lead singer of Talking Heads is more famous than Rob Thomas, the lead singer of Matchbox 20. If you were a teen in the early 2000s, the opposite might be true. How famous you perceive David Byrne or Rob Thomas to be is relative to when you were born, where you lived, and a number of other cultural factors.

If you're in the pizza business, you might consider the CEO of Domino's to be famous. (Carol's audience does.) You might instantly recognize his name or photograph. However, if you're in the soft drink or soda business, you might consider the CEO of PepsiCo to be famous. You might know her name off the top of your head. Industry Icons are famous relative to their industry. But ask someone in the construction business if they know who the CEO of PepsiCo is, and they're more likely to give you a blank stare. But they could tell you the name of the CEO of Caterpillar.

A friend or colleague may have forwarded you the link to the "Evolution of Dance" in 2006, but it's unlikely you knew the name of the dancer in that video.

In the speaking business, your level of fame is relative to three things: the event organizer, the audience they serve, and the other speakers they've hired in the past (or are currently considering).

Here's what we mean: if an event organizer hired Condoleezza Rice to keynote last year, and she's considering Judson this year, there's no doubt that Condoleezza Rice is more famous. However, let's imagine that the organizer's audience is two thousand YouTube influencers. Who's going to fill more seats: Condoleezza Rice, or The World's First YouTube Celebrity?

Fame is relative, but that doesn't mean you can't measure and understand where you fit in an organizer or audience's mind. It means you can use what you know about the organizer, the audience, and the other speakers they've hired to set your fee and emphasize your value.

Remember, in the grand scheme, the Fame Factor is a sliding scale from unknown to famous. But let's break it down even further.

There are three types of fame—three sub-factors you can adjust to increase your value to event organizers and understand your place in their world: worldly fame, domain fame, and fractal fame.

Worldly fame

Kim Kardashian, Magic Johnson, Michelle Obama, Gwyneth Paltrow, Colin Powell, Queen Latifah, and Will Smith are all worldly famous. They're in the Actors, Athletes, and Astronauts category. They're household names that event planners love for one simple reason: they fill seats.

Advertise and market the fact that Will Smith or Ellen DeGeneres is keynoting your annual user-conference, and many people will sign up without even considering the rest of the agenda.

When you're that famous, your demand for speaking engagements is so high you can charge (almost) whatever you want. Because your name alone fills seats, you command a higher price. Rumor has it that Will Smith's speaking fee ranges from $500,000 to $1,000,000, and he has earned it. Will Smith is worldly famous.

Think of it this way: if you don't need to read their bio or even their title to know who they are, they are worldly famous.

Few of us will ever be this famous. And you never actually need to be to have a thriving career as a professional speaker. But there are ways to dial up certain types of fame, because, although you don't need to have it to work professionally, there's a direct correlation between how famous an event organizer considers you to be and the fee you can garner.

Taken alone, worldly fame can give you (and the market) a skewed perspective of your value to the event organizer. That's why there are two other sub-factors that make up a total Fame Factor.

Domain fame

It's highly likely that others consider you to be an expert. Maybe they consider you a marketing expert, a sales expert, an HR expert, a leadership expert, an inclusion expert, or an innovation expert. Maybe others have referred to you as a thought-leader. All of that is great!

When others in a specified sphere of knowledge know you as a specialist in your field, they're helping to increase your domain fame.

Domain fame is not a measure of your expertise, it's a measure of the perception of your expertise.

We live in a world where anyone (and everyone) can call themselves an expert. Ironically, the true domain experts and visionaries rarely refer to themselves as such. Consistently earning a top spot as one of your domain's most-prized thinkers and speakers doesn't happen overnight. It takes challenging your domain's conventional thinking to separate yourself from the overpopulated world of self-appointed experts.

Generally, the more visionary your thinking, the more widely your ideas are consumed and shared, the more domain famous you become.

For example, Andrew Davis is considered a marketing thought-leader. He's appeared in thousands of blog posts, quoting his speeches, books, and ideas. Andrew's achieved some domain fame in the marketing sphere. However, Seth Godin is even more domain famous than Andrew, which is why Seth commands a higher keynote fee than Andrew.

As your domain fame increases, your name starts to appear on industry influencer lists with headlines like

"Top 10 HR Influencers to Follow on LinkedIn" or "Who's Who in Sales Enablement This Year"—and you're climbing the ranks of the elite personalities in your industry or area of expertise. As your speech evolves into a referable speech, you may start to see an intersection between your domain fame and your speaking experience. For example, you may pop up on lists like, "Top 20 Innovation Speakers You Must See" or "The Most Influential Personal Finance Speakers in the World."

Being domain famous reinforces your visionary status in a specific area of influence, which is fantastic. Event producers want to ensure they're providing their audience with game-changing insights from the most respected names in the industry.

For example, imagine the meeting planner in charge of an event for 750 heating, ventilation, and air conditioning (HVAC) contractors. She could hire a marketing speaker who's a self-appointed marketing expert (as evidenced by their title on LinkedIn). Or she could hire one of the "Top 20 Best Marketing Speakers" as evidenced by an *Inc.* magazine blog post. Who do you think is worth more to the event organizer? You guessed it, the one on the domain fame list.

Every expert fits somewhere on the domain fame scale, however, the most intriguing fame sub-factor is the next one.

Fractal fame

Worldly fame and domain fame are easy to explain. Fractal fame needs some additional context. Before we explain exactly what fractal fame is, we need to explain why we've chosen the word fractal, and why other words just won't do.

Remember Dr. Elliot Eisenberg? The entertaining economist who's taken advantage of his referral tree? He understands the power of fractal fame.

When it comes to the mortgage business or the credit union industry, Dr. Eisenberg is fractal famous: he's known by many in two branches of his referral tree. In the jobber market, there's only one economist whose event organizers call to speak at their events: Dr. Eisenberg.

We suggest you banish the concept of a niche from your mind and open it to the possibilities of fractals, by analyzing and expanding your referral tree. Dr. Eisenberg's referral tree is just a series of fractals he's managed to become famous in, and as you build a referable speech, you can intentionally grow your referral tree too.

It's much easier and more likely to become famous on one of the smaller branches of an industry than it is at the trunk of your domain.

Maybe you've found yourself speaking to audience after audience in the real estate business, even though you're a sales trainer. You might consider real estate a niche in which you've built a successful speaking business. But let's take a moment to dive a little deeper into the real estate business. There are commercial real estate brokers and residential real estate brokers. There are leasing agents in both commercial and residential real estate. There are real estate attorneys, and real estate software companies. There are real estate consultants and property managers. Talk to someone in commercial real estate sales and they'll tell you it's completely different from residential real estate sales. Talk to someone in residential sales about residential leasing and property management and they'll tell you it's a whole different ball game.

Now, you know, because you're a sales expert, that sales is sales. But that doesn't matter to an event organizer. They'd much rather hire a speaker who understands how "different" residential sales is from commercial sales (and they'll even pay more for that person).

The Referral Tree

EXAMPLE: REAL ESTATE

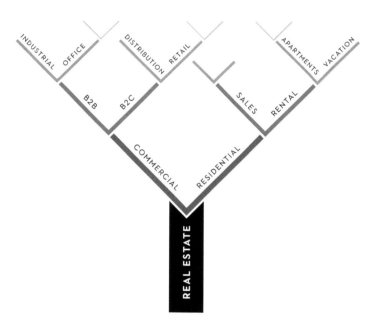

So, real estate might be a fractal on your referral tree. Every new branch is a new opportunity to make yourself more relevant to the branches that follow. Real estate might branch into two new branches: residential and commercial real estate. Those might branch into two more. And so on.

It's much easier to become famous on a small branch way up the tree and work your way down toward the real estate trunk than it is to become instantly famous there.

Instead of waiting for new stageside leads that unlock powerful new branches, take control of the branches you grow by implementing a simple, but strategic approach to increasing your fractal fame: divide and subdivide the potential markets you could (or do) serve until you find a branch small enough to build your fame rapidly, but large enough to build momentum around.

Phil M. Jones is known for inspiring audiences of salespeople to change the way they sell by learning "exactly what to say" (also the title of his bestselling book). Phil is a sales expert. There are thousands of sales training events and conferences every year, and those conferences are inundated with speakers who (on paper) look and sound exactly like Phil.

Phil knows that it's extremely hard to stand out in his industry.

So, instead of dividing the sales tree trunk into online sales and offline sales, Phil chose an entirely new tree, where not everyone is a sales trainer.

As a consultant, Phil had some experience helping a hearing aid manufacturer transform their sales experience. When Phil got booked to speak to one of the hearing aid trade associations, he unlocked an entirely new fractal: the hearing aid sales branch. Phil estimated that by January 2020, he'd spoken at over 150 events for hearing aid manufacturers, audiologists, and hearing screeners (those are even smaller branches of the same tree).

It's quite possible that your fractal fame is more important than worldly fame or domain fame to most meeting planners and event organizers. It's also the easiest to impact and enhance.

So many of us aspire to be considered a thought-leader in our own industry. Maybe you're a marketing expert and you'd love to deliver the keynote at Marketing Nation or Content Marketing World. Or maybe you're an HR expert and you dream of speaking in front of ten thousand people at the Association for Talent Development event this year. Right now, you're very likely thinking of your industry's most prestigious stages, and, sure, it would be great to speak at those events. But the fastest path to your speaking businesses success isn't necessarily on those stages.

Instead, find a branch in which there's a tremendous opportunity to build a healthy referral tree. That way, you can leverage your referable speech to reliably generate stageside leads. The amazing thing about fractal fame is that it happens rapidly and can continue to reap dividends for years.

Over a decade ago, Andrew Davis realized the home building industry needed some fresh marketing advice. The market was in the tank, marketing budgets had been stripped back to the bare minimum, and there were a ton of new houses on the market with no buyers. So, after speaking at the American Business Media conference in Charleston, South Carolina, Andrew struck up a relationship with one of the biggest home builder magazines in the world. In subsequent conversations, he worked to understand their challenges, learn their acronyms, speak their language, and then he offered his counterintuitive insight in a series of articles online.

Before long, the publisher of that magazine invited him to speak at a breakout session at one of their executive leadership events. That breakout session received such high praise that the event organizer brought him back to keynote the very same event the following year. A decade later, Andrew is still booking new gigs in the home building industry and has generated over $750,000 in speaking fees in this one fractal branch (and the related fractals). He's made himself fractal famous in the home building business. You can do the very same thing.

A word to the wise. If you're not intentionally choosing your fractal branches, you may find that a fractal will choose you. Certainly, that might work in your favor if it's a fractal that you love working with and it's also aligned with your brand identity, but you are known by the company you keep so choose carefully.

Shortly after Michael's first book, *Book Yourself Solid*, was released in 2006, he was invited to keynote a conference at full fee for an association that serves balloon benders, aka, balloon twisters or balloon artists. You know, those fine folks who create balloon animals and other twisted balloon sculptures at kids' birthday parties and street festivals.

Michael thoroughly enjoyed his time there, and, gauging from the audience's reaction, he nailed it. As a result, Michael blew up (we couldn't resist) in the balloon-twisting fractal. Within two days, he had two more stageside leads: full-fee offers to speak at other conferences for more balloon benders. Yes, Michael was as surprised as you are to discover that there is more than one association for balloon benders. But that's the point. These narrow fractal markets exist for almost every industry on earth. You could make a career speaking only to balloon benders all over the world.

Michael decided to let those opportunities float away because his demand at the time was so high he could dive into deeper fractals with higher potential. However, if Michael had wanted to continue to climb this tree, he likely would have found himself performing for other branches of fringe entertainers including, but not limited to, clowns, magicians, and mascots.

Nail a referable speech at the right event in a new fractal and suddenly you'll appear to be everywhere in that industry. You'll see an amazingly rapid increase in the industry's perception of your fame. You'll be covered in trade publications, featured on podcasts, see your insights quoted on industry blogs. Overnight, it appears you're everywhere. You'll suddenly be a big fish in a small pond others in your industry have ignored because they're so eager to speak at the most prestigious events in the industry.

Fractal fame increases your domain fame factor over time: the more fractals you penetrate over the course of your career, the more domain fame you earn. In effect, you're building your industry fame backwards—from outside of your industry in.

It's possible that you will earn worldly fame at some point in the future, but if you do, you'll be an outlier. Even Malcolm Gladwell isn't worldly famous like Will Smith. Nor is Brené Brown worldly famous like Ellen DeGeneres. Both Malcolm and Brené have about as much domain fame as one can have, but they are not household names. If you can safely walk into a mall without being accosted by a mob of adoring fans, you are not worldly famous.

It bears repeating: you don't *need* worldly fame to build a successful and long-lasting speaking career. Start by quickly increasing your fractal fame, and you'll chart a clear path to a calendar filled with full-fee gigs for audiences that eagerly anticipate your speech. Then, as you become famous in a number of fractals, you'll earn more domain fame. When you do, your fee will increase, and you'll have more requests to deliver your keynote than you have days available on the calendar.

The Fractal Fame Cycle

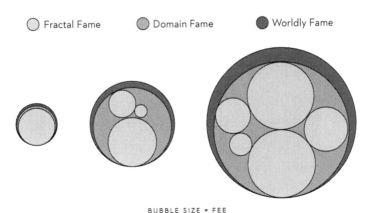

⬤ Fractal Fame   ⬤ Domain Fame   ⬤ Worldly Fame

BUBBLE SIZE = FEE

Remember when Judson Laipply said, "Fame is a funny thing"? Well, it is. As a Surprise and Delight speaker, you don't need to rely solely on your marketing, your accolades, your accomplishments, or the media coverage you garner to get more gigs. Instead, you rely on your ability to surprise and delight those in your session. Deliver a transformational experience they didn't expect, and you'll start moving up the Fame Factor ladders.

Instead of shooting for worldly fame, realize this: climb the ladder to fractal fame and you'll increase your domain fame. Max out your domain fame and you'll increase your worldly fame. Accomplish this challenge in multiple fractals across multiple domains, and now you're in Brené Brown and Malcolm Gladwell territory.

But fame isn't the only thing that meeting planners consider when determining who's best for their event. Let's dive into the second primary factor meeting planners evaluate when choosing a speaker: the Entertainment Factor.

CALLBACKS

- If you don't need to read their bio or even their title to know who they are, they are worldly famous.

- Domain fame is not a measure of your expertise, it's a measure of the perception of your expertise.

- It's much easier and more likely to become famous on one of the smaller branches of an industry than it is at the trunk of your domain.

- Increasing your fractal fame is as simple as dividing and subdividing the potential markets you could (or do) serve until you find a branch small enough to build your fame rapidly, but large enough to build momentum around.

- Fractal fame is more important than worldly fame or domain fame to most meeting planners and event organizers. It's also the easiest to impact and enhance.

- Fractal fame increases your domain fame factor over time.

(5)

The Entertainment Factor

OR MUCH of her speaking career, Kelsey Ramsden was a good speaker. Named Canada's Top Female Entrepreneur and the founder of several multi-million-dollar businesses, she booked big stages and netted respectable fees.

But something was missing. She could feel it.

For years, she winged her speeches, figuring that if she knew her content well enough, she should be able to deliver it well enough off the cuff. And she did.

She was funny and real, and audiences loved her for how she made them feel. In fact, she measured her success by how many "criers" were in the audience at the end of her often touching speech.

To Kelsey, though, that was the problem.

She knew she did a good job, but she wanted to be a world-class speaker, the kind who changes minds and persuades people to behave differently, not just in the moment, but beyond the event. She wanted to be a visionary, someone who is tapped to deliver memorable speeches again and again, not just someone who shares best practices and a few tips.

To create the referable speech that would put her in bigger rooms in front of larger audiences for higher fees, she recognized that she would have to make some major changes.

Earning a spot on the stage—any stage—is an honor (or, in Canadian, an "honour"). Kelsey could continue to deliver speeches in the same old "transactional" way, trading ideas for money and winging it onstage. She could get away with that—many people do—but not exactly honor her audience. Or she could choose to be an artist, a performer who creates an experience that feels more like a two-way conversation between the audience and the person onstage.

So, she enrolled in a comprehensive speaker training program at Heroic Public Speaking. Kelsey spent three months on scriptwriting and four months rehearsing the staging (her movement onstage, sometimes referred to as blocking). She also integrated the use, placement, and treatment of props and other set pieces. She upleveled the quality of her performance by adding theatrical elements and choosing how she wants her audience to feel, think, and act as a result of the actions she plays. Her training taught her how to be intentional in her movement onstage and add drama that makes the message more memorable and more impactful.

More referable.

She crafted remarkable micro-moments through signature bits, including leaving personalized fortune cookies under every seat in the audience. Instead of winging a perfectly adequate speech, now she delivers a carefully crafted performance.

And it's paid off. Since focusing on the referable speech, Kelsey has tripled her speaking fees and feels comfortable asking for more money because she knows she's delivering a one-of-a-kind experience. She's appearing before larger audiences, including her first stadium gig, for Sir Richard Branson's Haste and Hustle conference in Toronto.

All because Kelsey decided to stop speaking and start performing.

This is the choice you make when you decide to reinvest the time you could spend on marketing your personal brand in becoming a referable speaker. You're making a conscious choice to move from being a speaker to becoming a performer.

Kelsey is a Surprise and Delight speaker because she understands the power of the Entertainment Factor to drive stageside leads. Kelsey's focus on the speech moved her away from being a novice presenter and closer to being a transformational performer.

The Entertainment Factor is a continuum from *novice presenter* on one end of the scale to *transformational performer* on the other end.

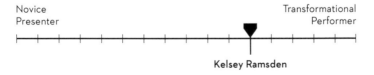

ENTERTAINMENT FACTOR

Novice Presenter — Transformational Performer

Kelsey Ramsden

A novice presenter shares information, thinking facts are enough to change the way people think and act. A transformational performer takes the audience on an entertaining journey that changes the way they think, act, and *feel*.

Here's the thing about entertainment: it's subjective and broad. And therein lies the opportunity.

What's funny, moving, or enlightening to one person might not be to someone else. Yet it's crucial to entertain. The kind of entertainer you want to be must fit with the kind of audience that you have now or wish to speak to in the future. It also must be true to you and your persona.

Some people come to professional speaking thinking they're already capable at performing. Or they know they have no idea how to perform. Whether you think you have it or think you don't, it doesn't matter, because talent is overrated.

If you don't learn how to leverage your natural talent to clearly express your ideas, you limit your growth. And if you *think* you don't have much talent, you can turn on the talent you do have through craft. You'll deliver more impact than those who have natural talent but lack the discipline to learn the craft of performance.

Most speeches are nothing more than narrated texts delivered from the stage by novice presenters. A meeting planner's agenda is packed with novice presenters. But when you make a speech entertaining, it becomes a *performance*. That's when you begin the transformation from speaker to performer.

A referable speech is a transformational experience, a performance made up of hundreds of micro-moments. It's not one monolithic thing delivered without contrast. When your content, and the way you deliver it, is all the same, it's monotonous. Monotony is boring. Boring doesn't book gigs or generate stageside leads. However, when you carefully craft, plan, plot, rehearse, and deliver a series of hundreds or even thousands of dynamic and contrasting moments with precision and excitement, you keep your audience on their toes and fully engaged for the length of your keynote.

In the thousands of hours we've spent chatting with event organizers and meeting planners, we've noticed that there are three things they look for in a great performance.

Signature bit: This is a section of the speech that's crafted and performed to drive home a point. It's so memorable that people go home and share it. They remember it. They talk about it. This is precisely *how* you get those stageside leads. It's similar to a funny bit a comedian does that people try to re-create for their friends and family, like Steve Martin's King Tut, Eddie Murphy's ice cream truck story, or Iliza Shlesinger "inviting a boy over." It's what sets apart a speaker's brand.

Reliable delivery: Spontaneity exists at the intersection of improvisation and preparation. That's why it costs thousands of dollars to buy a ticket to see *Hamilton*, and eleven bucks (plus two drinks) to go to a local improv show. *Hamilton* is going to work every time, but the improv? It depends on the night. It depends on the performers. It depends on the audience. Keynote performers deliver a choreographed performance so that meeting planners can trust that the speech they bought is the speech they'll get.

Reliable delivery creates consistency. When speakers wing it onstage, they don't deserve to be paid as much. The speaker who delivers a transformational performance every single time, without fail, deserves to be paid a lot more.

An experience: A referable speech is a theatrical experience. It feels less like a lecture and more like a show. Deliver a speech that changes the way the audience thinks, acts, and feels, and you've created a transformational experience. Craft a performance and you'll change the way people feel about themselves, see the world, and operate in it. Instead of receiving feedback like, "Thanks, I learned some good tips and tricks," people will say, "You've changed the way I see the world," or "My mind is blown. I'll never be the same person again."

In order to earn your spot onstage, you'll need to move from speaker to performer. If you're relying on a catchy open, a smart close, and some PowerPoint slides to get you through a forty-five-minute virtual keynote or a main-stage presentation, you need to stop speaking and start performing.

And it all starts by crafting a signature bit. After all, your bit is designed to get people talking about your performance. That's what generates those stageside leads.

The signature bit

Eliot Wagonheim has long known that most people do not want to spend an hour listening to a lawyer talk about contracts. The problem is that he's a lawyer who talks about contracts.

Eliot's always been a better-than-average speaker, honing his skills before judges, juries, arbitrators, and fellow attorneys at lunch-and-learn events. He is a skilled writer and a formidable teacher, breaking through the legalese to make sense of the law for laypeople and peers alike. For the most part, his audiences have always given him good reviews.

Yet onstage, he had a tendency to pace, so he tried to distract the audience from his unsettling habit by making fun of himself. Deep down, he knew he wasn't serving his audience as well as he could. He gave an information-rich speech, but not really an effective performance. He needed to upgrade his performance skills.

He made a choice to move beyond simply writing out a speech (which is still more than most take the time to do). He'd mark up those scripts by highlighting the operative words that gave every sentence its meaning. He'd denote the significant changes in pacing or pauses he needed to hit for dramatic effect. Eliot got better and better.

But it was his next transformation that catapulted him from being a good speaker to becoming a sought-after performer: he started testing signature bits.

In one speech, he pantomimed walking on a tightrope. In another, he kicked off his speech with a rap. Then he landed on Superman. At least, that's what audiences call his signature bit involving, of all things, a perfectly appropriate display of disrobing onstage.

To demonstrate to business owners at an engineering firm that you don't have to be a lawyer to understand contracts, Eliot took the stage dressed like a buttoned-up lawyer and soon took off his jacket... then his tie... then his dress shirt... until he was standing before them in khakis and an Under Armour shirt. Instead of just talking about contracts, he transformed into dressing like his audience to amplify his message about the universality of contracts.

At one of his workshops, an attendee asked, "Are you going to do your Superman thing?" His "Superman thing" had become the signature bit that made him stand out from other speakers. This signature bit made his speech and his message so entertaining and memorable, that he was soon hired to give ninety-minute workshops on contracts to sixteen of his client's regional offices nationwide. As a result, the firm became his biggest client.

Eliot's Superman bit made his speech and him relatable, memorable, and referable. It also made him hirable.

It's not as though Eliot knows the law better than every other attorney. Rather, he can give a performance that his clients will remember. Best of all, when he finishes his speeches, his audience wants more—from a lawyer, of all people.

A SIGNATURE BIT is a piece of educational content performed with theatricality that solidifies a speaker's brand. It supports a big idea. It's memorable and repeatable.

An effective signature bit is:

* **Transformational**: the audience is changed in thought, words, and/or actions.

* **Insightful**: it shines a light on a hidden or new idea or thought process.

- **Provocative:** it highlights extremes or provokes the audience by challenging traditional narratives or long-held beliefs.

- **Unique:** something that only you do in a way that only you can do.

- **Memorable:** if it's transformational, insightful, provocative, and unique, it's highly likely that it will also be memorable.

Every speaker can benefit from a memorable signature bit because it helps audiences relay the big idea of the speech to other people in an entertaining and, therefore, referable way.

The Signature Bit Effect

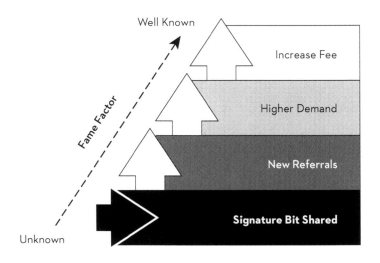

They can't repeat all forty-five or sixty minutes of your speech, but they can share your signature bit. It helps them articulate your message to show how transformational, insightful, or provocative it was. Plus, it allows them to relive the moment, bringing them back to the experience and how it made them feel, think, or act.

Signature bits get shared. Sharing then drives referrals. Referrals increase demand. Increased demand raises your fee. A great signature bit doesn't just deliver you more stageside leads, it increases your Fame Factor. Because a signature bit is specifically designed to be talked about by those in your audience, it inherently increases your fame. In today's always on, social media-driven world, a great signature bit can even reach an audience well beyond a single performance.

Remember Judson Laipply's "Evolution of Dance" and its viral video explosion?

That dance *is* Judson's signature bit, and it's not part of his speech because it went viral on YouTube. It's the other way around. The dance went viral because it is part of his speech.

Judson's six-minute dance routine is—and always has been—the finale to one of his most-booked speeches, "Life Is Change." The dance is a metaphor for how change is constant, but we evolve with it. The dance *is* the message. It's a performance that transforms the way the audience sees change.

Signature bits aren't easy to craft. They take time. They require inspiration and thought.

Judson had been working hard to find a signature bit since 2000, when a speaking mentor told him he needed a *thing*. "You have to do something no one else does," his mentor, David Coleman, said. "It has to be unique to you. So unique that if someone says, 'have you seen Judson do his thing?' the only person to have done that would be you."

David Coleman also has a signature bit that kills on college campuses. Every. Single. Time. David is known as The Dating Doctor, and his signature bit is hilarious. In just a few minutes he riffles through a dozen bad kissers. If you ask a college event organizer if they've seen the "Bad Kissers" speech, they know exactly who you're talking about. Judson needed his "Bad Kissers" thing, and he knew it.

For months, Judson searched for his signature bit. Until, one day in 2000, at one of his college gigs, a comedian took the stage.

"He did a really funny five-minute set about how people dance at weddings and bar mitzvahs. He even mimicked some of the dances like the YMCA and the Electric Slide," Judson recalls. "It came to me in a flash." As soon as the comedian left the stage, Judson shuffled out of the event venue and went back to his hotel room.

A half-hour later, he'd written down the first twelve dance moves and started stringing them together in his mind. A few weeks later, he'd taught himself how to mix music, and he'd rehearsed the dance hundreds of times.

He debuted his new dance medley at the end of his speech at a regional showcase for college speakers. It killed.

Immediately after the show, his manager came backstage and said, "Holy cow! That's your *thing*!"

For five years Judson tweaked it. Changed it. Grew it. Honed it. He rehearsed it. He hustled nonstop growing his business through referrals who knew him as the "Evolution of Dance" guy.

Remember those kids who emailed Judson almost every day for a month asking him to upload the video? The ones whose constant pestering would turn Judson into a YouTube celebrity? Those kids hadn't seen the dance at a talent show. They'd seen Judson perform it during his keynote at a LEAD Conference with a thousand other high school students.

Those kids loved Judson's signature bit so much they wanted to perform it at their high school talent show.

Judson is proof that if you focus on your speech, your signature bit can become your greatest marketing asset, increase your fame factor, and make you highly referable.

Want to create a signature bit? Make big choices

The best-known signature bits come from great comedians. Ellen DeGeneres became famous after her appearance on *The Tonight Show Starring Johnny Carson* when she performed her "Phone Call to God" bit. It earned her the coveted invitation to sit at Carson's desk after her routine, a treat bestowed on only a few comedians, who often went on to successful comedy careers. In recent years, though, Ellen's signature bit hasn't even involved words: she dances. For years, she's opened her show by dancing across the stage and through the audience. It's become such a big part of her public persona that people ask her to dance with them as they're walking down the street. It's memorable and repeatable and lots of fun. It's even provocative, because Ellen gets strangers to dance in public and on camera.

Now more than ever, the performance skills that speakers use are compared to those of comedians and other performers. While a decade ago, you pretty much had to go to a comedy club or catch a few TV specials by the biggest name comedians on HBO or Comedy Central to take in a comedy show, now you can watch hour-long stand-up specials anytime you want on Netflix or Amazon by nearly any comedian with a following. Where comedians used to deliver a series of one-liners, now they're change agents, offering an overarching message for a purpose.

Think of the long-form comedy programs of recent years: Hannah Gadsby's *Nanette*, Hasan Minhaj's *Homecoming King*, and Trevor Noah's *Son of Patricia*. They're not just trying to make people laugh. They're trying to change the way people think, and maybe even what they do, in transformational, insightful, and provocative ways. As a result, they've raised the expectations for all sorts of performances, including professional speaking.

But you don't have to be a comedian to have a signature bit. As a bestselling author and top-tier speaker, Brené Brown knows how to use a signature bit to drive her message forward. In her Netflix special, *The Call to Courage*, which is her keynote speech, she tells the story of swimming in a lake with her husband while on vacation. She uses the moment to try to connect with him, but he rebuffs her... and she gets ticked off. So she makes up stories as to why he was being so standoffish—things having to do with her and how she looks in a Speedo, for instance. Only after they have a fight about it, does she discover the truth: he was having a panic attack in the water.

The signature bit is rooted in the way she tells the story, drawing us into her way of thinking and her point of view until she turns it all on its head with the reveal of her husband's truth. It supports her message about the courage to be vulnerable despite the stories you tell yourself. It's insightful and transformational because it gets you to think differently and, perhaps, act differently too.

Carla Harris, vice chairman, managing director, and senior client advisor at Morgan Stanley, always takes the stage wearing a magnificent string of pearls. It's not until she gets to her signature bit that you realize that the string of pearls isn't just a great fashion choice. Carla's signature bit reveals the pearls of wisdom she's uncovered working on Wall Street for three decades. It's more than a pun, it's a memorable statement about her success and what we can all learn from it.

Just like great musicians have their signature songs—such as Led Zeppelin's "Stairway to Heaven," Lizzo's "Truth Hurts," and Garth Brooks's "Friends in Low Places"—great speakers have signature bits. They need them to drive home their message.

Scott Stratten's signature bit, "Millennials Don't Know Our Pain," pokes fun at millennials, Generation Xers, and baby boomers alike. It's fun and funny, because millennials will never know what it's like trying to download forty-five minutes of music on an MP3 only to have Mom pick up the phone and ruin the download. But it also supports his big idea: that millennial bias (or any bias) hurts us all. His signature bit gets shared by audience members retelling it and through video clips shared online. It's memorable, repeatable, and makes him stand out from other speakers sharing similar messages, by being provocative, making fun of several generations at once. Scott Stratten's viral video of his signature bit also increased his Fame Factor.

Bobby McFerrin, made famous by his successful song "Don't Worry, Be Happy," has created a signature bit designed to demonstrate the power of the pentatonic scale to his audience. It involves singing and jumping onstage, but with his exceptional performance skills, it's so much more than that: He assigns musical notes to a stage-wide pretend piano, jumping on certain "keys" to elicit the correct note as vocalized by the audience. It's memorable. It unites and connects the audience to him and one another. They become part of a larger experience, rather than just witnesses to an idea presented onstage. It transforms the audience through a provocation that says, "Here, let's sing together."

A signature bit can have action and spectacle, like Olympic hurdler Sarah Wells teaching kids to overcome obstacles by leading them to hurdle each other on the stage. It can offer a sense of awe, such as Jill Bolte Taylor holding a human brain and spinal cord during her TED Talk, "My Stroke of Insight," to illustrate the effects of her brain injury. It can have emotional resonance, as in Martin Luther King Jr.'s "I Have a Dream" speech.

A signature bit could even be content found in the public domain and then turned into something uniquely yours— as long as it's material that you legitimately, legally, and ethically have the right to use. Early in his speaking career, Michael Port repurposed an age-old Aesop fable dating back to the sixth century BC called "The Man, the Boy, and the Donkey" to create his own signature bit. The result is an old story that, as always, ends with the donkey drowning, but with a moral that has a new twist: instead of the classic, "Please all, and you will please none," Michael ends with, "If you try to please everyone, you might as well kiss your ass goodbye." It's insightful, memorable, repeatable, and pretty darn funny when delivered with perfect timing. What's more, it makes one of his big ideas—that you'll be a more effective thought leader if you're fully self-expressed rather than constrained by your fears of what other people think—more tangible.

Your signature bit is personal; only you can give it. While anyone can perform the Aesop fable, they cannot do it quite the way Michael did to make it his own. No one else could do Brené Brown's swimming bit, Bobby McFerrin's pentatonic scale bit, or Scott Stratten's millennials bit quite like they do. They can try, but it won't be the same.

A signature bit is ordinary content turned into memorable, transformational, and shareable content through a one-of-a-kind theatrical performance.

Often, a world-class speaker spends the most time preparing and rehearsing the signature bit, which may make up just five minutes of a speech—it's that crucial to the delivery of the message. Effective speakers lean into the theatricality of the bit. Their motions, movement, emotions, and actions are deliberate. And they're willing to be a little wrong (provocative) to be so very right (insightful and transformative).

When NSA Hall of Famer Jay Baer began working on his "Hug Your Haters" speech, he wanted to share a few online reviews for various businesses. He'd put the reviews on the screen and turn away from the audience to read them. It didn't quite work as well as Jay would have liked, though, because he was reading it at the same time as the audience, who may read more quickly or more slowly than Jay did. So the punchline rarely lined up. What's more, the delivery didn't have much theatricality to it.

As he worked through the signature bit with Michael and Amy Port at Heroic Public Speaking, they suggested using voiceovers by character actors for each of the rather scathing, yet funny reviews. When he plays the reviews during his keynote, audiences eat it up. They get the jokes at the same time. The idea makes it a good concept, but the delivery makes it a signature bit.

In 2008, Andrew Davis needed to illustrate how people really search the internet. So, instead of showing some stats or slides supporting how the web has changed how we buy, he crafted a signature bit designed to show the audience. Over the course of seven minutes, Andrew takes the audience on a hilarious journey that starts with looking for a picture of meatloaf and ends with two tickets to a Meatloaf concert. Over a decade later, event planners still request his Meatloaf bit.

Some speakers worry about giving away their slides when people ask for them. But when you have a polished and practiced signature bit, no one can take your slides and present your speech quite like you do. It just won't work as well. When you have a solid signature bit, you won't mind giving away your slides. In fact, you may find yourself using fewer slides, because you no longer need them.

Joey Coleman swapped out a slide of a scared kid on a roller coaster, which he used to show how he felt as a child, and replaced it with a physical signature bit that worked well when delivered by Joey, whose face is as expressive as Jim Carrey's. Anyone could use a slide, but only Joey could perform the bit. He no longer needs to use slides for his signature roller-coaster bit because the humor now comes from him rather than the slides. However, he has another signature bit that closes his speech using seventy-five slides in four minutes to review the entire speech. Those four minutes culminate in a mic drop moment and a standing ovation. Again, anyone could use his slides, but only Joey can do the bit.

Creating a signature bit requires you to make big choices.

One of the biggest choices you have to make is whether or not you're willing to be fully self-expressed. The signature bit helps you bring more of yourself (which really means bigger choices) to the presentation because really, that's what audiences want.

When Olympian Sarah Wells first worked with Michael, she wore high heels, a pencil skirt, and a fancy hairdo, but it didn't match her persona of an Olympic athlete. It simply wasn't what the audience was looking for in an elite-level athlete talking about overcoming life's hurdles.

So Michael encouraged her to kick off her high heels, change into running gear, and start jogging around the stage to get moving and feel more like herself. Initially, she was a bit skeptical about Michael's suggestion to have her hurdle over him. But when it was a hit with the six hundred audience members observing her training, she knew she had to incorporate it into her speech. Since then, she's encouraged audience members to come up onstage, form a line, and hurdle each other. It's now her signature bit.

Once she stopped constraining herself to what she thought she *had* to be and instead brought more of herself to the stage, she became a unique, compelling, and relatable performer with her own style and sensibility.

For five years, superstar speaker Ron Tite has performed and perfected a signature bit about shampoo. Lots of it.

While staying at the Westin Grand in Vancouver, he tweeted, "I love the Westin Grand." They tweeted their love back for him and asked if there was anything they could do to make his stay better. So he reported that there was no shampoo in his room that morning. The hotel responded by delivering a personalized note with some goodies, which he went on to talk about on social media and in his speeches.

So when he returned to the hotel the next time he was in town, he got yet another set of goodies, his favorite snacks—Diet Coke and barbecue chips—and, wait for it … twenty bottles of shampoo. Also, a framed photo from his Facebook page of him with his dogs, along with a personalized note wishing him a stay that feels like home.

The purpose of his bit is to illustrate how important it is to have a genuine desire to connect with other people in business. He uses it in different ways for different audiences, dialing up or toning down certain aspects of the bit to fit the message for the event.

For Ron, it's important to keep perfecting the bit and trying new things because sometimes he stumbles on something that adds to the core of the bit or develops into a new bit altogether. It's also important that the bit never feel old or overdone for him. In fact, he's retired bits for that very reason.

One of Ron's bits about lost luggage on Air Canada was so popular he felt the need for something fresh. And when somebody addressed him as the "Air Canada guy," he knew it was time to put that bit out to pasture.

When you're ready for a new signature bit, it's time to explore. Or as Ron says, "Pan for silver and work for gold." If you don't continue to strive for signature bits, mining for new material, aerating and amplifying it, you'll never succeed at creating them. It's the constant pursuit of stronger material that makes for a better speech. Don't be afraid to go after it. Nor, when necessary, to tweet for more shampoo.

Your signature bit sets you apart. However, if you don't deliver it (and the rest of your speech) with consistency, all that work crafting something worth referring to is wasted.

That's why meeting planners look for all the markers of reliable speech delivery.

Reliable delivery

Rachel DeAlto once offered ten different speeches about relationships on the college speaking circuit. Actually, it was more than that, because she'd take on any topic the meeting planner asked for and cram it into her speeches. As a result, her sessions weren't much more than a series of thoughts delivered via microphone.

"One meeting planner wanted me to talk about Title IX [a law that protects people from discrimination based on sex in education programs or activities]. Only, I'd have to learn about it to teach it," she says. So she did.

Rachel wasn't sharing her expertise so much as delivering whatever was asked of her, like she was the short-order cook of speakers. Then she got a wake-up call from a friend, an accomplished speaker who asked, "What are you really good at?"

Rachel could speak about a variety of topics, but it all came down to one overarching theme: relatability. So she abandoned her list of speeches and created one keynote with four key parts that never change and smaller parts that can be tailored to each audience. She went from being a short-order cook to being a chef with a set menu and a couple of specials.

Rachel's new speech was a hit. So much so that her referral tree grew outside the college market and suddenly corporate audiences were hiring her. She can still tailor her speech for a predominantly male audience of facility managers or a female audience of corporate executives.

Her reliable delivery of one keynote speech helps people understand quickly what she speaks about, and that adds to her referability. She's increased her speaking frequency to twice a month (twenty-four gigs per year), including large keynotes at conventions. What's more, she used this speech to test material for a new book.

Even her feedback has improved. "Before, they'd say, 'I liked Rachel. She's great,' like they want to have a beer with me," she says. "Now they say, 'My employees need this' or 'My leadership team needs this.'"

That's because with reliable delivery, she now has a referable speech.

Your audience can tell if your speech is off the cuff. Even if you're a subject matter expert or you can jog your memory with your slides, event organizers can tell the difference between winging it and a well-built performance.

Maybe the speaker is furtively glancing at the "confidence monitor," or looking down to decide what to say next (hoping the words will be written on the floor?). Maybe they stumble through their slides on a virtual event. They might repeat themselves, pace onstage, hold a handful of notes, read off their slides, or clutch the podium. They might suddenly speed through material or run out of things to say because they've misjudged the amount of material needed for the time allotted. Toward the end of a speech, maybe you've heard a speaker say something like, "If you remember anything, remember this one thing..." Or, "If I had more time..." Or, the worst for all involved: "Oh, they're signaling to me to wrap it up..."

These are all clues to an audience—and most importantly to meeting planners—that the speaker is hoping the speech will go the way they'd like, but they're not sure. It wasn't well rehearsed. Even if the speaker does a good job, even if the audience likes the speech, it's less likely someone will refer the speaker to another meeting planner because it's not obvious that they can do it again in the same way. They may be able to deliver most of the same information again, but they can't necessarily reliably deliver the same experience again.

Reliable delivery is one of the keys to crafting and delivering a referable speech.

People who are reliable are typically considered more trustworthy because trust is based on making commitments and fulfilling them. If you're able to fulfill the commitments that you make to the meeting planner and to the audience by producing a consistent experience, it makes your speech a lot easier to refer. Everyone understands that you'll deliver this caliber of speech each and every time.

For example, Bruce Springsteen may change up his setlist gig to gig, but he delivers each song and the overall performance reliably and consistently because he and the E Street Band have rehearsed and performed them over and over. His fans know they'll get the same reliable delivery at every concert, and, most likely, "Born to Run."

If you think the top performers can just skip rehearsal and dial it in, think again. In Beyoncé's Netflix concert special, *Homecoming*, she gives us a behind-the-scenes look at how she prepared for her headline performance at the Coachella Valley Music and Arts Festival. She and her crew spent four months rehearsing the music and another four months rehearsing the dance numbers *just for one event*.

Beyoncé says people don't like to rehearse because it requires them to be humble. Sweaty from dancing and still carrying extra weight from her pregnancy with twins, she says, "You gotta be willing to look awkward, and you gotta study. You gotta be a student."

If Beyoncé thinks she needs to rehearse, but you think you can deliver best-in-class performances worthy of top-dollar fees by winging it, you might have some kind of superpower mere mortals (like one of the bestselling artists of all time worth north of $500 million) could only dream of.

Truth be told, the bar for speakers is remarkably low. Many speakers wing it, use slides to provide content, pay no attention to their movement onstage, and haven't actively identified how they want their audiences to feel at any given moment in their speech.

When you're starting out, it's tempting to take whatever speaking opportunity comes your way and to promise to customize your speech to each event. But doing too much customization can set you up for inconsistent and unreliable delivery, making it less likely to secure a stageside lead.

Time and again, we've seen how reliable delivery advances a speaker's career.

Antoine Dupont admits that when it came to giving speeches, he used to be a "circus monkey," performing whatever the meeting planner asked him to do. The night before a speech, he'd throw together some slides based on speeches he'd delivered before about marketing and whatever was in his brain at the moment—and then change the slides an hour before the event.

He'd lead with a bit that he knew would make the audience laugh because he had long been a natural storyteller, even if it didn't support the theme of his speech. More or less, he'd wing it onstage, and he thought it worked. Sort of.

Now, however, he's a "recovering professional winger," delivering prepared, rehearsed, and tested keynotes. Well, at least eighty percent of them are. He says he's still working on his delivery, fine-tuning his signature bit and teachable moments. But now his speech has a clear structure, purposefully placed beats (pauses), and deliberate staging that aligns with what he's saying.

He cites his new training in scriptwriting and stagecraft skills from HPS and his work behind the scenes as much as on the stage as the keys to his rising success. He tests material with an online rehearsal group and even onstage with an in-person rehearsal group that he hosts at a local theater a few times a year. He says feedback from trusted peers, who have the same training in stagecraft—the technical aspects of theatrical production including movement, props, choreography, music, character, language, audience interaction, surprise, tempo, spectacle, drama, multimedia, lights, story, staging, rhythm, revelation, suspense—is crucial.

Professional speaking can be a lonely pursuit. But there's no quick fix to reliable delivery. You have to put in the time and make continuous improvements.

The result is amazing value and reliable delivery. Meeting planners have said so, and it's gotten Antoine referrals for other keynotes. It's also poised him to consider doubling his rates as he fast becomes "the best $5,000 keynoter east of the Mississippi." Now that he understands the power of a reliably delivered session, he is worth more—much more.

Reliable delivery makes you a safe referral for meeting planners and audiences alike.

Reliable delivery trumps customization. Every time.

What?

The Paradox of Customization

Sure, theoretically, customization can be an effective technique for creating an experience that is relevant and personal for an audience. You can even have a go-to speech that you customize, as Ann Handley did. But if you can't customize and deliver it reliably, it's not going to make your speech more referable. In fact, it'll interfere with your ability to book gigs.

We call this the Paradox of Customization, and it's a trap that many speakers fall into when they plan their speeches. Why?

Customization gives speakers an excuse for winging it. If you don't have a planned, rehearsed, and reliably delivered speech, you might lean on the idea that it's because you do more customization than others. So, instead of front-loading the hard work of producing a best-in-class keynote you might, instead, try to customize each speech you give. In theory, it's admirable, but, in practice, it's usually counterproductive, ineffective, laborious, and even fool-hardy, because you can't guarantee the effectiveness of an untested speech. Reliably delivered sessions generate more stageside leads than a speech you wing.

Speakers often rely too heavily on customization as a sales technique. We get this. You want to demonstrate that you're going to add a lot of value to the event by speaking directly to the unique needs of the client. However, this approach suggests that your work, as it stands, won't add value without being changed for their benefit. Your speech shouldn't need dramatic customization to deliver what you promise and what the audience needs. So many speakers spend hours learning acronyms, doing industry research, or talking to corporate executives so they deeply understand their client's needs. However, sometimes this undermines one of the primary reasons speakers are hired: precisely because you're not from their industry and they want an outside perspective. Moreover, when you attempt to customize every speech you give, you may come off as someone who is trying just a bit too hard to make it seem like you know as much about their world as they do.

Speakers are often worried that audience members may have already seen their keynote and will be put off if the content is the same. If that's true, then the organization shouldn't have hired you for this presentation. If you don't have another keynote that you can reliably deliver, avoid the temptation to say yes because you want the work. Instead, refer them to another speaker (speakers get speakers work). Problem solved. It's also possible that the meeting planner wants you back to deliver the same speech because they loved it so much the first time. In fact, audiences often enjoy it the second time even more because they go into it with a better conceptual understanding of the key points. On the second go, they may be able to better consume the nuances you reveal. So, while meeting planners may want your session to be "tailored" to their audience, they don't want that tailoring to compromise your reliable performance.

Recently, one of us referred a speaker to an event planning company that produces almost all of the big events for an entire industry, but they didn't hire the speaker. When we asked why, they confessed: "Well, we went online and watched a number of their keynotes, and each speech seemed so different that we didn't know what we'd get if we hired them."

Think about it: If a planner is responsible for a big event with so much at stake, they are looking for safety first.

They want a Surprise and Delight speaker: a speaker who surprises the audience but *not* the event organizer. They don't want you to play it safe in your approach to creating a transformational experience for their audiences. But they do want to feel safe in the knowledge that you'll be able to deliver exactly what you say you'll deliver.

Remember, most organizers have either seen you speak before, or someone they trust has seen you speak before. That's precisely *how* you got the gig. Don't let them down by changing all the things they loved about your session the first time they saw it.

The Goldilocks Principle

The solution to the constant customization of your speeches is to use a modular approach. Some portions of the speech are always the same and other sections are always tailored to the audience. The goal is to tailor just enough of the content to be relevant, but not so much that it compromises your performance. We call this the Goldilocks Principle.

Perhaps the beginning, the end, and the signature bit always stay the same while the tailored portions are your teaching points. You may swap out one rehearsed story to illustrate your points to a tech audience and swap in another story for a group of nurses. Or maybe you tailor your list of tips one way for human resources professionals and another for C-suite executives.

All of the critical elements of the speech from a structural, educational, and delivery perspective are already dialed in. That way, you don't have to come up with a new signature bit for every speech. You tailor other, smaller portions and deliver the speech in repeatable and reliable ways because you're never starting from scratch.

If a modular approach sounds too square for you, maybe you'd like to take the donut approach to tailoring your content for meeting planners: You can craft and rehearse short segments in which the setup and payoff are always the same, but the examples you use to support the point are industry-specific. It's called a *donut* because there's a hole in the middle of the short segment that must be filled with new content each and every time. When you use a donut, the transitions and flow of the speech stay intact, it's the hole in the middle that changes. Your speech may have three donuts that total only twelve minutes of content, but that's plenty of tailoring, and you know it can be delivered reliably.

The Donut Recipe

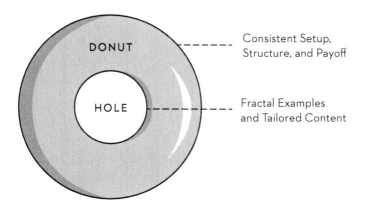

DONUT — Consistent Setup, Structure, and Payoff

HOLE — Fractal Examples and Tailored Content

When you start your speech with a wandering and wordy warm open followed by an, "Okay, let's get started," that's not exactly confidence-inspiring. It usually means you haven't prepared well enough to know how to get into your speech. Then you might take five to ten minutes warming up before your speech starts to take off. But you don't really have that luxury.

If you want more of those stageside leads, you'd better grab the audience's attention from the start, inspiring them to listen because you're clearly prepared. Audiences recognize that they're not listening to a lecture; they're witnessing a performance and having an experience.

The stage isn't the only place to inspire confidence though. The Goldilocks Principle applies to the marketing of your speeches too.

According to NSA Hall of Famer Scott McKain, "Mediocre speakers have ten topics. Good speakers have five. Great speakers have no more than three." Even three speeches can be overkill. Go to any speaker's website—if you see a large number of speech offerings, experienced meeting planners are less likely to take them as seriously.

Speakers at the top of their game generally market one speech at a time. Perhaps that corresponds with a book, and they do it well for a number of years until they write a new book and then a new speech. Other speakers perform the same speech for a decade, making improvements along the way.

Andrew Davis is still giving a speech he originally wrote a decade ago; however, he doesn't market that speech anymore. It's not on his website. He doesn't actively sell it. He's only still delivering that speech because he's still getting stageside leads every time he performs it.

If you're a new speaker and you ask us how many speeches you should offer, we'll likely answer with some sass: "Well, you can sell and deliver as many speeches as you want. As long as it's no more than one."

But, once you've been in the business for a number of years, the answer will change slightly because the Goldilocks Principle suggests that you should offer as many sessions as you need to stay relevant, but not so many that you appear to be all over the map.

Remember, the referable speaker is constantly making a choice: they choose to focus on the speech instead of the marketing. Of course, the choice is yours. You can choose to do a lot of work coming up with titles and descriptions for many different speeches but do very little work on the actual speech. Or you can focus your efforts on giving one referable speech, reliably delivered.

We trust that you'll make the wise choice.

The secret to reliable delivery

Tuesday night at Sally O'Brien's in Somerville, Massachusetts, is open mic night. Every week for two years, Andrew showed up along with two-dozen-or-so other wannabe comedians and signed up for a five-minute slot onstage.

It wasn't long before Andrew became friends with a comedian who'd been trying his material out at the very same bar for three years. Josh was funny, but he was still working up to a mediocre five-minute set.

Week after week, Andrew and Josh would rework their routines. Refining one or two jokes at a time, always trying out new material. They'd compare notes or offer each other suggestions after they got their five minutes onstage, then they'd try it again next week.

It's a slow, slow, slow, process.

One day, the host of Sally O'Brien's open mic night announced that he'd no longer be able to host the comedy roundup. "Does anyone want to take over for me and host this every week?" he asked the room.

Josh's hand immediately shot up. "I will," he shouted.

"Sucker," the rest of the room thought to themselves.

"Josh," Andrew whispered, "what are you doing? Hosting this thing is awful. You have to stay all night, every week, listening to bad jokes from people who aren't serious about their comedy. Why are you volunteering?"

"Because I need more stage time to get better, faster, and who has the most stage time every week? The host," Josh said as his hand still flailed in the air.

Andrew scoffed.

Over the next nine months, Andrew watched Josh perfect joke after joke after joke. You see, between each comedian, the host gets two or three minutes onstage. So in one night, instead of one five-minute slot, Josh got thirty-five or forty minutes total.

Some Tuesdays, Josh would just rework one little bit over and over and over as people meandered in and out of the bar. Other nights, he'd try all new jokes. Josh got ten times the amount of stage time Andrew got every single month, and it showed. His comedy got better and better, faster and faster.

In nine months, Josh had a full fifteen minutes of perfectly timed, hilarious comedy, while Andrew had three mediocre jokes.

Josh understood the Law of Iteration, which states that the quality of your idea increases exponentially each time you share it.

By the end of the year, Josh had moved to New York City, and he took his fifteen-minute set to comedy clubs every single night. Before long, scouts from *Conan* saw Josh's set and invited him to appear on the show.

Today, Josh Gondelman is one of the most sought-after comedy writers in the world. He's won five Emmy awards for his writing on *Last Week Tonight with John Oliver*, written two hilarious books and countless articles for some of the most prestigious magazines in the world, released two comedy albums, and commands top dollar for a full hour of comedy at colleges and universities around the country.

When Josh decided to leave Sally O'Brien's for New York, he got up onstage and asked the same room the very same question we'd all heard nine months before, "Does anyone want to take over for me and host this every week?"

No one raised their hand. No one. Not even Andrew.

It took Andrew another decade to embrace the Law of Iteration. Not only does the quality of your idea increase each time you share it, but the more rapidly you deliver and hone your message and your performance, the faster your speech improves. The faster your speech improves, the sooner it'll become a referable speech. Remember, your speech's referability is directly proportional to the speed at which it evolves.

Don't wait. Iterate.

The secret to giving a referable speech is the preparation. Preparation takes rehearsal. It takes iteration. The secret to reliable delivery isn't a secret at all. It's just misunderstood.

We rarely meet speakers who rehearse as much as they need to. Why not? Some speakers say they don't like rehearsal, that it doesn't work: "Well, I did some rehearsal, and then when I got onstage, I just felt stiff, and I couldn't remember what I'd rehearsed. I wasn't quick on my feet, and that's usually my strong point. It just didn't work."

You know what? They're one hundred percent correct: their rehearsal actually interfered with their ability to perform. But it's not because they did *too much* rehearsal. It's because they didn't do enough.

Instead of being in the moment onstage and allowing the material to come to them organically and quickly, like a natural thought, they have to think. They actually don't know the material well enough. That's why some people believe that rehearsal doesn't work. But it's actually *not enough* rehearsal that's the problem.

Other speakers say, "Well, if I'm really well rehearsed, and I have to deliver the speech as planned, how can I be spontaneous?"

Spontaneity lives at this intersection of preparation and improvisation.

When you're so prepared that your speech comes to you organically and in the moment, you'll earn the ability to go off script as needed—*and* come back to the script effortlessly. When you know your material inside and out, backwards and forwards, you'll have stellar situational awareness. It's as though you can see yourself perform *while* you're performing.

So, when something unexpected happens, you're unfazed. You're able to play with the disruption through improvisation and then pick up exactly where you left off. It appears effortless.

Enough rehearsal leads to lower anxiety. Sure, it takes a while to achieve this level of situational awareness, but rehearsing gets you there.

We're not talking about just memorizing your speech. Reading your script over and over again out loud is not an effective way to rehearse. It may help you remember the words, but that's not rehearsing, that's memorizing. Effective rehearsals require you to feel like you're onstage delivering what (and how) you intend to.

If you're going to be able to deliver an exciting experience for five thousand people on a stage that's 250 feet wide with a 250-foot LED screen behind you, you'd better have some sort of proficiency or mastery, and that takes time and preparation. Or, if you're delivering a virtual session to three hundred people you can't see or hear, you'd better be ready when the tech goes on the fritz.

And, by the way, pacing the length of your hotel room while you mutter your material is not rehearsal. It's mild-anxiety management.

Running through your materials in your head while riding the elevator is not rehearsal. It's high-anxiety management.

Logging on fifteen minutes early to make sure your camera and mic are working for your virtual keynote is not a rehearsal. It's a tech check.

Doing a cursory reading once or twice before you deliver the speech is not rehearsal. It's just a run-through.

Clicking through your slides over and over so that you make sure your transitions are working properly is not rehearsal. It's a deck check.

Most of what speakers do to work on their speeches is about managing nerves rather than improving the speech incrementally over time.

So many speakers resist the sometimes arduous and uncomfortable rehearsal process. But why? Why wouldn't you rehearse if you know it's good for your reputation, your audiences, and your bank account? If you know that rehearsal is good for you, why don't you do it regularly?

We believe there are two possible reasons: one, rehearsal is uncomfortable and messy, and two, you just might not know how to do it well.

Let's start by looking at the discomfort that is often a part of the rehearsal process. Remember what Beyoncé revealed: "You gotta be willing to look awkward, and you gotta study. You gotta be a student."

Rehearsing is hard and messy. Most of the choices you make in rehearsal don't work the first time you try them, or the second, third, or even the fourth time. Sometimes it takes four weeks or more of daily work on one bit before it starts to take shape.

If you were to map out the yield curve on the rehearsal process, this is what it might look like when working on improving a bit.

The Breakthrough Chart

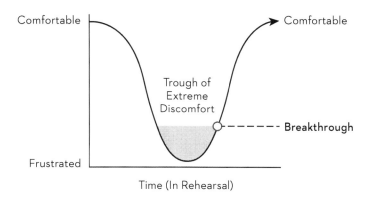

It's comfortable at first, but as you break down a story or a bit and try small new things to improve it, it gets more and more uncomfortable. Oftentimes, the bit even gets worse. (It can be soul-crushing.) Congratulations, you've just entered the Trough of Extreme Discomfort.

At this point you have two options: Go back to what you were doing before (which will feel very comfortable). Or break through the discomfort and continue to refine and rehearse until it gets better, feels comfortable, and works better. Those who break through create a new normal. They set the bar higher with a new level of comfort and a better performance.

The people who don't break through and just go back to what they were doing are the very same people who say, "Well, I did some rehearsal, and then when I got onstage, I just felt stiff. Rehearsing doesn't work for me."

You've got to break through the Trough of Extreme Discomfort and then keep working up the curve. Those speakers who consistently generate three, four, or five stageside leads from every single gig have done it. But how?

Think about it this way: when you're only tweaking thirty or forty seconds of your speech every time you deliver it, it might take you ninety gigs to rework your entire speech (and that's just one tweak for every thirty seconds). If you deliver twelve gigs a year it will take you over seven years to overhaul your speech. That's why some say it takes years to become a referable speaker. That's why they say you've got to put in the reps.

There's a better way. Get comfortable being uncomfortable when you're *not* in front of an audience, and do it often.

On February 13, 2009, a month before releasing his first book, Anthony Jack took the stage to address the American Academy of Arts & Sciences and share the most compelling findings from *The Privileged Poor: How Elite Colleges Are Failing Disadvantaged Students*. His message is compelling. His voice is mesmerizing. His presence is commanding, and his prose is elegant. But Anthony's reading from a script and is anchored to the podium behind which he stands. He's so comfortable there that for much of the fifteen-minute speech he has one hand in his pocket; despite his ease, it feels like an academic treatise.

About three months later, a very different Anthony Jack takes the stage at TEDx in Cambridge, Massachusetts. He is holding no notes. There is no podium to anchor himself to. His hands are free to move as he dives right into a hilarious anecdote about his first visit to Amherst College.

Anthony is mesmerizing! The audience eats up every one of the twelve minutes of his speech. It's not rushed, and he looks more comfortable than he did giving his February speech. Anthony had broken through. He got comfortable being uncomfortable. Anthony built a reliable speech, and he rehearsed his way there.

What's more important, being comfortable or getting results? Sometimes the most meaningful way to live is to stop taking the easy way out and do what's good for you. Maybe asking and answering that question will motivate you to commit to doing much more rehearsal in service of your career and the needs of the people you serve.

So, how do you rehearse?

If you're starting a brand-new speech, you'll spend a significant amount of time on the ideation, content development, and scriptwriting. Then you'll move into a scheduled rehearsal process that might run from six weeks to six months. This is very similar to the way that a director and actors would approach the rehearsal for a play. It's a detailed and involved process. And it works. The 7-Step Rehearsal Process is designed to help you work on a new speech from concept to opening night.

Michael Port dedicated a comprehensive chapter to the 7-Step Rehearsal Process for a new speech in his book *Steal the Show*, a *Wall Street Journal* bestseller. So we're not going to re-explain it here. Instead, we're giving you access to a video of Amy Port, cofounder of Heroic Public Speaking, teaching the full 7-Step Rehearsal Process. To watch it, go to TheReferableSpeaker.com.

Now, how do you rehearse if you're already delivering a speech?

Since a speech is never "done," you can continually iterate. Not thirty seconds at a time, but major pieces of the entire speech. That should instantly feel uncomfortable. Let us introduce you to the 5-Minute Method.

This rehearsal process lives between the comedian's approach to tweaking small things each and every time they perform and the 7-Step Rehearsal Process to rehearse a brand-new speech.

The concept is simple. Take five minutes of your speech, and rework it.

- Rework how you move (the blocking).
- Rework what you say (the script).
- Refine your storytelling.
- Clarify your main points.
- Add contrast (the peaks and valleys that break up your speech).
- Add drama and tension.
- Adjust your timing.
- Rethink your pacing.
- Get *uncomfortable* with all the changes you're making.

Then, stand up (yes, even if it's a virtual presentation) and deliver those five minutes with exacting precision until it starts feeling comfortable. This will take days, but you're exponentially increasing the reliability of your delivery, and you're doing it faster than it would take to make one tweak at a time.

Once you've pushed through the Trough of Extreme Discomfort on that first five-minute chunk, add another five-minute segment.

To see exactly how the 5-Minute Method works, watch the video of Andrew detailing the process at TheReferable Speaker.com.

One of the most effective ways to kick off this approach is to rewatch your most recent speech. Go back to a recording of your latest virtual presentation, or film your next in-person gig (even shoot it on your phone). Now sit down and rewatch the entire session. Yes, this will be uncomfortable, but that's the point. Take notes. Lots of notes. Watch the speech as if you're in the audience. Be hyper-critical of even the smallest things. Take notes of the areas that lag. Listen to the audience's reactions.

If it's a virtual keynote and you have access to the live chat, read every single message the audience members post. The watch-party situation created in a virtual environment provides you with one of the most valuable insights into the audience members' minds.

Is a question asked at a specific point in your presentation that you don't answer? Take note. Is the audience quiet for minutes at a time? Write that down. Could the audience be confused if they are asking for the slides? Be vigilant and dismiss nothing. Make no excuses for any reaction to your session, your style, even your appearance. Everything matters.

Now, select the five minutes that you feel needs the most attention and start reworking it. Start from the ground up. Get the five minutes you've selected from your recorded speech transcription now and start re-scripting.

Once you've revised the script, stand up and start rehearsing just those five minutes. Your objective is to make clearer choices that produce a better experience for the audience from both educational and entertainment perspectives. Each new choice should raise the stakes of your performance by focusing on what you want audience members to think, do, and feel.

Take nothing for granted. Be ruthless. Be thorough. Be thoughtful. Be intentional. When you push through the Trough of Extreme Discomfort for the first five-minute chunk and you're back in the comfort zone, select another five minutes.

Now, film and watch your next performance and the audience reactions. After ten gigs or so, you'll have an entirely new and improved speech.

Rehearsal is not just about repetition. Repeating a section of your speech without adjusting it doesn't make it better. The premise is simple: consistently improve your speech and you'll get booked more often. Get booked more often and you can constantly raise your fees and reach more people.

Rehearsal is the only time-tested, honest path to making massive leaps in your entertainment factor. Ignore it and meeting planners will ignore you. Give it the attention it deserves, and you'll earn the attention and fees you deserve.

Remember, your speech is never done. A referable speaker is continually improving their speech by using the 7-Step Rehearsal Process when they embark on a brand-new speech, the 5-Minute Method for making big improvements on one small piece at a time, and the comedian's approach to continuously refining their performance.

That's the recipe for reliable delivery, all designed to create a unique experience for the audience. And it's the experience that changes lives.

Creating an experience

Erik Wahl has performed his keynote onstage in front of 27,000 people. It's a one-of-a-kind experience that capitalizes on his history as a businessman and his skills as a visual artist. Today, he's one of the most sought-after corporate speakers, precisely because he doesn't just deliver a speech. Rather, he creates an amazing *experience*. But the magic doesn't start onstage. It begins before he gets there.

For Erik, creating his performance looks like this.

He ships his equipment, including easels, paints, canvases, and even his clothes to the event in advance. He brings a producer with him to his speaking events to oversee his video and visuals while he's speaking and painting onstage. He also brings multiple printed copies of the slides for the crew to follow so his team is clear on the show's goals.

His producer calls the show for him, handling the placement and advancement of his slides and video on big LED screens behind him. Cameras follow him onstage to capture him while he paints, and he even talks to the cameras, creating a very dramatic event. It's like you're watching the creation of a stylized movie about the creative process in real time.

He even gives away the paintings he creates to the organization that's hosting the event, and they put them up in their offices, so his art becomes part of their company culture.

Creating such an experience for the audience, the meeting planner, the AV crew, and the company holding the event requires planning, rehearsing, coordinating, stagecrafting, and repeatedly delivering the same level of experience. In short: He's mastered his ability to reliably deliver a great experience. It's high-level stuff, and if you're aiming for the top end of the meeting planners' speaker budget, you need to learn how it's done.

Top-tier speakers like Erik are top-notch teachers who use theatrical elements to help audiences consume and then act on their educational content. That includes stagecraft, which should be part of every keynoter's vocabulary. If you want to evolve from delivering speeches to performing experiences, think about how you can use stagecraft and who it will benefit.

You might think only the audience experiences a keynote, but don't forget the meeting planner or the speakers' bureau, not to mention your fellow speakers. What about the tech crew and the decision-makers at the organization hiring you? When you create a speech with all of these players in mind, you begin to understand why it's crucial to deliver an experience, not simply a keynote. All of those people also generate stageside leads.

Clint Pulver understands stagecraft too.

Clint goes beyond the usual keynote the moment he sets his drum kit onstage. A professional drummer, he brings his musical talents to corporate and education audiences to teach them how to create lasting loyalty. In his interactive keynotes and workshops, he even invites audience members to use drumsticks to make music on upside-down plastic buckets—and they do.

But his creative teaching methods aren't limited to the stage. For some clients, he uses a hidden camera—with the company's permission—to create an "Undercover Millennial" video, asking young employees about how they feel about their work. The result is an honest, uninhibited look at what the company needs to improve. Then he shares the video during his keynote, blurring out the employees' images onscreen. Clint provides the company with a valuable service that exceeds the capabilities of an employee survey, and he packages it as a performance.

Maybe you're thinking that getting props, like drums and buckets, to an event is too much trouble, but remember: Beyoncé brings eighteen-wheelers full of equipment because she's delivering an *experience*. Even Ed Sheeran, who keeps his shows about as simple as possible, has to get his guitar to his gigs. That's because they're performers, and you can be too. It just takes some creativity.

Even adding just one prop to your keynote can make the big idea of your speech stickier. Fighter pilot Tammy Barlette uses a deactivated 30 mm round of ammunition from the Warthog fighter jet to illustrate her point about social courage.

Sometimes it's not a prop that creates an experience. Marcus Sheridan arrives early to every gig and spends much of his preshow time meeting people in the audience so he can memorize their names and then address them personally from the stage. Marcus has trained himself to do this, and it surprises and delights every attendee and meeting planner, every single time.

Joey Coleman goes even further by looking up audience members on Facebook and LinkedIn before he arrives at the event. Then he incorporates those audience members onstage using their LinkedIn profiles and social media pages. It looks and feels spontaneous, but he's putting in the research and effort before the event, for the event. (By the way, Joey and Clint both use the donut method for tailoring their sessions.)

How could you turn data into a fascinating audience experience? NSA Hall of Famer and *New York Times* bestselling author Sally Hogshead created a test to measure a personal brand's most fascinating traits. Before her corporate gigs, each audience member takes the Fascinate® Test and receives a custom report pinpointing their most impressive qualities, with titles such as The Evolutionary, The Scholar, The Connoisseur, and The Diplomat.

Then, in her presentation, Sally showcases charts and graphs of the audience's aggregate data, revealing their hidden communication patterns. Audience members can compare themselves to their coworkers and leverage their unique value. Sure, it takes research and a team to support this level of service, but the audience members gain a new understanding of themselves and each other, and that's an experience worth having.

It is this kind of attention to your audience's experience that makes them feel like they're watching a *show* rather than just a speech from a talking head.

In the virtual world, the idea that the audience is watching a show isn't a metaphor, it's a reality. So when Andrew Davis found himself confined to his home during the COVID-19 pandemic, he literally transformed his keynote presentations into a fifty-one-minute video experience.

Where did he find the inspiration? Television shows, which are usually forty-six to fifty-one minutes long. And audiences noticed: "[Andrew Davis] is like the Alton Brown for marketing. Innovative presentation format (and great thinking)," tweeted Ann Gynn (@AnnGynn).

The idea of using stagecraft to deliver an experience isn't limited to the in-person experience. As Andrew discovered, there are things he could never do onstage that he can do in the virtual world. Things like leaving the virtual "stage," taking his audience on a journey to buy a car, or slicing a pizza in the kitchen to demonstrate the fragmented marketing landscape. Andrew built a lightboard to illustrate complicated concepts. All of his ideas he's borrowed from television. It's liberating. It's exciting. It's an experience.

Andrew produced a video series on rethinking virtual events. You can watch all four parts at TheReferable Speaker.com.

Transformational experiences

When the educational and the theatrical elements of a speech are in perfect balance, your speech delivers a transformational audience experience. Too many educational elements without any stagecraft, emotional resonance, or excitement, and you tip the scale toward a typical high school lecture. Bueller? Bueller?

If a speech is all theatrics and stagecraft but lacks the substantive, relevant, educational elements, the audience may leave thinking, "Holy cow, that was entertaining. I mean, I have no idea what that was about, but it was fun."

It's like watching performance art that is too conceptual to be transformative, or attending a motivational speech that leaves you feeling fired up for a bit but a few hours later you find yourself watching TV and cracking open a pint of Ben & Jerry's Chunky Monkey.

If you're not at least thinking about how you might be able to use these tools, you're missing an opportunity to raise the level of your performance and the experience for your audience.

Transformational Audience Experience

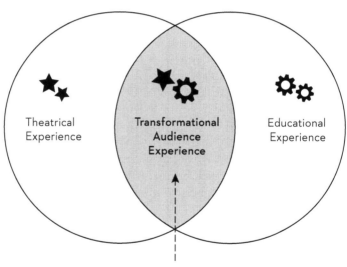

Slimming your slide deck

Theo Tsaousides, PhD, says that reading dense copy and then switching gears to listen to a speaker is "cognitively taxing." And he ought to know. Theo is a neuropsychologist.

Despite knowing they were cognitively taxing, Theo prepared customized decks of copy-heavy slides, complete with tables and charts, for his talks. He'd even make tweaks to his slides right up to the moment he took the stage. After all, that's how it's often done in academia, where conventional wisdom is that reading from your information-rich slides proves you're an expert.

It took Theo years to realize that when he watched other speakers' presentations, he found their slides distracting. That's when it clicked. He's not onstage to read slides. He's there to provide a transformational experience. So he decided to try something completely out of the ordinary for academia: he slimmed down his slide deck. Then he did it again, and again. The decks got slimmer, and the content on each slide, shorter. Soon, he was relying on his performance skills instead of his slides.

That turned out to be a fortuitous decision.

At one of his speaking gigs, a mortified and panic-stricken event planner rushed up to Theo seconds before he took the stage to tell him that she'd misplaced his deck. Theo was thrilled. Finally, he had an excuse to deliver his presentation without a single slide.

She eventually found his slides and projected them onto the screen behind him. But Theo had already connected with the audience. He'd made a joke about being nervous to present without slides. He took a sip of water, then joked that it wasn't water at all but the potent Greek liquor ouzo (if you can't tell from his name, he's Greek too).

Theo realized something immediately: "They were engaged, like they were having a conversation with me," he told us.

He still uses slides now and then, but they act as visual support for his message instead of a crutch for his content. When Theo shows his audience two slides that dramatically illustrate one of his points, they usually let out a collective "Whoa!" Theo (and his audiences) have discovered that even seemingly tedious research data can be presented in an interesting and memorable way.

Theo no longer creates copy-heavy slide decks that sit in the drawer after each customized speech. Instead, he modifies portions of one well-rehearsed speech that he delivers reliably and repeatedly. It's paid off, too, with referrals for additional keynotes, workshops, and individual and group training.

"My ideas are better illustrated through me than through a slide with a table on them," he says. "I've discovered that you have to be able to deliver the experience even without all the 'stuff.'"

To be clear, we're not saying that you *should* or *shouldn't* use slides or other visuals. Far from it. What we're saying is that if you rely too heavily on slides or, worse, lean on them as a way to deliver your keynote, you're likely *not* delivering a referable speech.

Speaking is a creative act, and there isn't only one way to do it. A gentleman summed up this perspective when he posted on Facebook, "My two favorite speakers are Seth

Godin and Michael Port. Seth because he can do a forty-five-minute speech with just a couple of stories and a hundred slides, and Michael because he can keep you on the edge of your seat for ninety minutes with no slides."

Being able to deliver your entire presentation without slides is a challenge. But it's one worth taking on. Because, like Theo knows, there are times when your slides go down, the guitar gets flown to the wrong city, and the dancers call in sick, but the show must go on. You may just find that you don't need the slides, and that is liberating.

At the most fundamental level, if you can't deliver your speech without your slides, you're not ready to speak professionally. Visuals can aid, but they don't replace. Finding the right balance between educational components and theatrical elements helps make your speech transformational. And transformational speeches are referable.

But wait, there's more. Yes, there's always more.

Earning trust and creating safety

Whether you're presenting virtually or in person, the right kind of audience interaction at the right time can help transform an audience. Unfortunately, it can also have the opposite effect.

Imagine you work for a large company and this year's all-hands annual conference features a personal finance speaker who opens his speech by demanding that you "raise your hand if you're in debt." To your left is your boss. To your right is a peer. Sitting in front of you is the new intern. Behind you is the CFO. How would you feel about revealing this kind of personal information in front of these four people, not to mention the fifteen hundred others in the room?

The audience doesn't feel safe enough to answer that question honestly.

Or, let's imagine you're watching a prerecorded virtual presentation, streamed as if it's live, to 150 software sales-people. The presenter invites the audience to share their latest sales objection in the group chat. "Maybe you've heard the product is too expensive or it's missing a specific feature? Go ahead, type in your most recent objection right now," she says.

The speaker pauses for a few seconds (nowhere near long enough for anyone to even think of an answer). "Alright, those are great! All those objections you just entered in the group chat, we're going to address in today's session," she says enthusiastically.

"What objections?" you think.

The audience no longer trusts the speaker or the experience.

If, like the personal finance speaker, you ask audience members to publicly answer highly personal questions, they're probably not going to feel safe, and that will affect the experience you're trying to deliver.

If, like the virtual presenter, you haven't completely thought through the audience's experience, your audience interaction may have the complete opposite of the intended effect.

You don't craft a transformational experience by simply asking for raised hands, forcing inauthentic interaction, borrowing clichés, or performing inauthentic tricks. (This includes the once popular, "Do you agree? Say yes or yes.")

Instead, build trust and create a sense of safety.

In Benjamin Zander's popular TED Talk, he persuades the audience to sing classical music notes with him. It's masterfully executed, and the audience loves it. How does he do it?

As the conductor of the Boston Philharmonic Orchestra, Benjamin first demonstrates the transformative power of classical music with an entertaining and humorous display of how children learn to play classical piano at various ages. It's endearing, funny, and smart. Then Benjamin plays a series of classical music pieces we all recognize to show the audience how much they actually know about and appreciate it. Only then does he encourage the audience to sing along. He's nearly halfway through the performance before he asks the audience for any interaction. Why wait so long? Because, first, he must earn the audience's trust.

When you're creating an experience, the amount of audience interaction you request should be proportional to the amount of trust you've earned.

Jane McGonigal is a game designer. Her TED Talk, viewed online by more than six million people, is a masterclass in audience interaction.

Instead of explaining how gamers feel when they're immersed in a game she's designed, Jane creates an experience that allows every single member of the audience to feel those emotions. How does she do it? Jane manages to pull off a massive multiplayer thumb-wrestling match. But you can't pull off that kind of experience without first creating a sense of safety for the audience. So Jane invites three volunteers to the stage to demonstrate the game and kick things off. By the end of the demo, the entire audience of fifteen hundred attendees is encouraged to join in. And they do.

It works because it's not a gimmick. Her massive multiplayer thumb-wrestling match *is* the experience. Her message is the ten emotions the audience feels in just sixty seconds.

Kate O'Neill, one of the first hundred employees at Netflix, and now a speaker who focuses on human-centric digital transformation, has received positive feedback for making the virtual experience more interactive while still being content rich. For example, during a recent virtual presentation for Google, she didn't have access to a chat feature. However, since there was a Q&A-based tool on the audience side, she restructured her content to build in pauses every fifteen minutes to give the client contact a chance to read her the questions that had come in. It facilitated a more interactive session than a traditional ninety-minute lecture would have. Within minutes of closing the presentation, Kate was pleased to find that she had messages waiting for her in her inbox from Googlers with follow-up thoughts, questions, and opportunities, making it a referable speech. She shared with us: "I'm finding more and more that people love when you go out of your way to show that you're including them in your presentation."

When delivering virtual presentations, Patricia Bravo, a speaker who brings a neuroscience-based approach to leadership, also switches interactive modalities approximately every fifteen or twenty minutes. She'll ask participants to drop a word in the chat to describe a feeling or respond to a prompt. Before her presentation officially begins, when participants join the webinar, she'll place them in randomized breakouts to best mimic peer conversations when entering a room in person. She'll also set up virtual breakout rooms where participants can move from room to room at will, giving them a feeling of autonomy and control. Often she'll enable the whiteboard feature in breakout rooms for participants to spotlight their ideas and debrief others on insights they're having during the presentation. When the participants are all in the main Zoom room, she will prompt them to turn on or off their video camera as a way of responding to a question: "If you've had this experience, turn off your camera for five seconds." It's simple but offers a powerful visual of social proof and encourages participation and engagement.

Consider trust and safety first, before you add any audience interaction element to your speech. Resist the urge to ask your audience to do something or say something they're not primed for. Without earning the audience's trust and creating an environment of safety, your audience interaction is trite and inauthentic. Instead of connecting with your audience, you're creating conflict by attempting to force an outcome. You're destroying the experience instead of enhancing it.

A meaningful experience doesn't feel gimmicky, and it isn't patronizing to the audience.

The right audience interaction techniques deliver emotional and structural contrast. They have the power to break through audience indifference and create a shared experience. They also make a performance more memorable. Memorable is referable.

You're not happy to be here

The audience's experience of you and your speech starts well before you take the stage. Well before your bio is read. It starts as soon as the event organizers announce that you've been booked to speak. Your photo, session description, and pre-event video promotion begin to set the tone for your speech, sculpt the attendees' expectations, and tease the experience that is to come.

And then ... the moment you take the stage, the audience sizes you up, attempts to determine whether you'll bore or entertain, bewilder or enlighten. Will you surprise and delight them?

How you start your speech is crucial to the experience.

A pleasant but irrelevant filler like, "Good morning! I am so happy to be here!" doesn't actually create connection. ("I am so happy to be here" might be the most common opening line at every event we've ever attended.)

You're *not* happy to be there.

What's the alternative? You're disappointed to be there? Let's assume that everyone is happy to be there and we don't have to acknowledge it.

Then there is the off-topic story or joke that doesn't land or fuel speech. These are the dad jokes of the speaking world. You know, jokes like, "I just flew in from Boston. Boy, are my arms tired!" Wah, wah.

There's also the tried and true: tell them what you're going to tell them, tell them, and then tell them what you told them. "Here's what I'm going to talk about today..." (Insert agenda slide here...) Boring.

You've only got a few seconds, maybe a minute, to prove your experience is going to surprise and delight the audience. Don't squander this time. Instead, take the audience on an exciting journey, a journey they want to see unfold.

Of the thousands of speeches we've experienced, we've only seen one performer, Hannah Gadsby, surprise and delight an audience using the "tell them what you're going to tell them" open. In her Netflix special *Douglas*, she delivers a hilariously killer keynote where she brilliantly sets expectations for what's to come. (Every speaker should watch it—it's a masterpiece.)

Here's the key: Hannah Gadsby doesn't use the "tell them what you're going to tell them" open and then drop it. Hannah brilliantly weaves her opening through the entire Netflix special.

So, remember: it's not just how you start a speech that solidifies your referability. How you end it is just as important, if not more so, than how you start. You want the audience to feel different when you step offstage or hit that red *Leave Meeting* button.

We've found speakers spend a disproportionate amount of time on their speech's opening rather than their closing. Maybe they think, "If I can nail the opening, I'll get into a groove and everything will be fine after that." But audiences tend to remember two things: the moment in the speech that elicits the most emotional response, no matter where it falls, and the very end of the session.

Closing with "Oh, well, I guess I'm out of time..." makes your performance feel unfinished, and your audience may feel cheated. Saying things like, "There's so much more to this presentation—if you have questions, I'll be here all day" doesn't leave an audience feeling confident that they've had the full experience. There is no more to your presentation. It's the end. Craft an experience that buttons it up and leaves them surprised and delighted.

Winston Churchill said, "If you have an important point to make, don't try to be subtle or clever. Use a pile driver. Hit the point once. Then come back and hit it again. Then hit it a third time—a tremendous whack."

Finding the right balance between your educational content and your theatrical elements will help you craft a transformational speech. Transform how the audience thinks or acts, and you'll increase the number of stageside leads.

Whack!

CALLBACKS

- Your speech's referability is directly proportional to the speed at which it evolves.

- A referable speech is a transformational experience, a performance made up of hundreds of micro-moments.

- A signature bit is a piece of educational content performed with theatricality that solidifies a speaker's brand. It supports a big idea. It's memorable and repeatable.

* A signature bit transforms ordinary content into transformational and shareable content through a one-of-a-kind theatrical performance.

* Your signature bit can become your greatest marketing asset, increase your fame factor, and make you highly referable.

* Reliable delivery is one of the keys to crafting and delivering a referable speech.

* Spontaneity lives at the intersection of preparation and improvisation.

* When you're creating an experience, the amount of audience interaction you request should be proportional to the amount of trust you've earned.

(6)

The Expertise Factor

—————————

JAY ACUNZO used to do exactly what event organizers asked: provide the audience with actionable take-aways they can implement when they get back to their desk on Monday.

Sitting in the audience of four thousand people watching the keynote at one of his industry's most prominent events, Jay thought: "I'm just as good. Why are they on the mainstage while I'm speaking in one of fourteen concurrent breakout sessions after lunch?"

Later that day, Jay delivered his breakout session full of meaty tips and tricks on how to be a better marketer. He knew he'd nailed it. The audience ate it up. They took snapshots of his slides. People came up afterward to tell him how great his session was. Other attendees stopped in the hall to thank him for all the hacks and tips he'd presented. At cocktail hour, he felt overwhelmed (and even slightly embarrassed) by all the compliments he received.

A few weeks later, the speaker evaluations came in:

"Clear and practical."

"Useful, passionate, engaging."

"Great tips & great energy."

"Concise, thoughtful, well presented."

Jay scored 4.82 out of 5. "Surely this will earn me the mainstage next year," he thought.

At Content Marketing World (CMWorld), you have to earn the keynote stage. Every year the conference organizers offer the highest-rated breakout session speaker the opportunity to deliver the opening keynote presentation the following year. It's a strategy designed to increase the quality of the breakout sessions by dangling a massive keynote as a reward for a stellar breakout session. For the second year in a row, Jay dreamed of being that speaker: the previously unknown breakout session plucked out of obscurity and thrown onto the mainstage in front of four thousand people.

Jay waited patiently for the phone call that would invite him to be the opening keynote speaker for the following year. The call didn't come.

Jay was devastated. All signs had pointed toward success: stellar comments, a high session score, the accolades that poured in during cocktail hour. "I deserved that keynote," Jay thought. However, not one to wallow in despair, Jay went back to work.

At the next year's CMWorld, Jay's breakout session was a hit: 4.9 out of 5 this time. Statistically, almost the same. There was one thing that was dramatically different from the previous year—the evaluation comments. This year they read:

"Jay NEEDS to be the 2017 keynote opener."

"KEYNOTE OPENER! ONE OF THE BEST OF THE CONFERENCE!"

"Incredible content! Incredible speaker & presenter. My favorite session by far."

"Great session! Would be an awesome keynote next year."

"Clever, funny, high energy, and incredibly informative. Loved this session."

"Blown away! He'd be a perfect inspirational closing keynote next year."

"Best talk at Content Marketing World by far."

"Best speaker of the entire event."

Three months later, the call came: "We would be honored to have you keynote next year's conference."

Jay Acunzo did it. He'd earned the keynote stage, and he'd received a bunch of inquiries to deliver the same speech from CMWorld at other events around the country. For a fee!

Jay went from breakout rooms to keynoting small events. Then he graduated from keynoting small events to more significant events. His referral tree flourished. When Jay walked onto the stage at CMWorld to deliver the speech he'd spent two years refining, he wondered how it could get any better.

It did.

That one keynote earned him dozens of other stageside leads. Not because Jay was famous, not just because he's entertaining, but because the right people in the audience loved the speech.

When you compare the audience evaluation comments Jay received at the very same event one year apart the difference is striking: "Clear and practical" versus "Blown away! He'd be a perfect inspirational closing keynote next year." And, "KEYNOTE OPENER! ONE OF THE BEST OF THE CONFERENCE!"

How exactly does a speaker go from well liked with a warm audience response to an over-the-top home run in one year? It's not like Jay Acunzo suddenly hit the best-seller list and increased his Fame Factor. Jay rehearsed (a lot), and, sure, he worked hard at being entertaining. But none of those things fully explain Jay's ascension to the key-note stage.

There are two things Jay understood and embraced that earn him exclamatory audience evaluations written in all caps.

Jay earned his spot as a Surprise and Delight speaker, not just because of the way his speech is performed, but because of the expertise he demonstrates and who it's aimed to reach and the kind of insight he delivered.

The Expertise Factor is a continuum from *subject matter expert* on one end of the scale to *visionary leader* status on the other end of the scale.

EXPERTISE FACTOR

Jay Acunzo

If we're to make sense of Jay's transformation from breakout presenter to keynote speaker, the first thing we'll need to break down is the Audience Hierarchy of Needs.

The Audience Hierarchy of Needs

It's easy to look out at an audience and think of it as a homogenous group. However, a referable speech and the speaker delivering it must be fully aware that every audience member is unique. They're attending your session with a specific set of challenges, a unique lens, given their position within their organization.

Most event planners ask for an assurance that you're going to deliver "actionable takeaways." They often tell you to make sure the audience "can get back to the office and implement three or four things right away." They're not wrong. Some of the people, the vast majority of audience members, want actionable takeaways. But not everyone.

Meeting planners rely heavily on audience surveys to dictate their attendees' desires, and after decades of reading session evaluations it's clear where the requests for actionable takeaways come from: those surveys.

It's been our experience that very few executives take the time to fill out audience feedback surveys. Very few CEOs download those event apps and check in to the sessions they attend. In effect, event planners get a skewed perspective of their audience's needs.

When it comes to building a fast-moving, ever-growing referral tree, you need the right people to invite you to speak. You need C-level executives watching your sessions and immediately seeing the need to have you speak to their organization. That's exactly the goal Jay met in his new speech. Jay didn't stop delivering actionable take-aways. Instead, he made sure his content spoke to everyone (including the very few executives) in the room.

The highest-quality referrals are top-level executives, which means we must speak to their needs without ignoring the other audience members in the room.

Let's break down the Audience Hierarchy of Needs from the bottom up:

The Audience Hierarchy of Needs

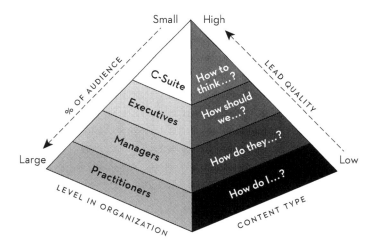

PRACTITIONERS: "HOW DO I" CONTENT

Practitioners are actively engaged in the day-to-day activities at an organization. If you're speaking to a hospital group, this might be the nurses and physicians actively seeing patients. Maybe you're speaking to a group of heavy-equipment dealers; your practitioners might be the people selling, marketing, or building the equipment every day. Practitioners actively fill out those audience feedback forms, and these are the people who need the tips, tricks, hacks, and how-tos. These people are actively looking for ways to enhance their day-to-day activities. Practitioners make up the vast majority of the audiences we serve.

Jay's first speech spoke directly to the practitioners in the room, and you can see it in the feedback: "Clear and practical." "Useful, passionate, engaging." "Great tips & great energy."

Practitioners are the lowest-quality referral. Why? Because they first try to implement the things we teach from the stage. It may take months before the practitioner realizes they need us to come and train, teach, or preach to the rest of their team. At this point, they have to sell us up and into the organization (a slow, tough process). They first have to convince their boss, and then their boss must convince their boss. Then that boss is tasked with finding and allocating the budget and convincing the rest of the executive team. It takes time.

You must address the practitioners' desire for "actionable insight" during your presentations, but you must not pander to them. You cannot focus solely on the practitioner if you want your speeches to earn those stageside leads for more keynote speeches.

MANAGERS: "HOW DO THEY" CONTENT

One tier up on the Audience Hierarchy of Needs are managers. Managers spend their days in charge of the activities, tactics, and training of the practitioners. Instead of the direct practical advice and insight their teams require, a manager is looking for "how do they" content. They want examples, case studies, best practices, lists, and guidelines that help them understand and manage their teams better. Managers expect to hear advice and insight from others in their industry: how do managers just like us, serving clients just like ours, implement your recommendations?

Managers aren't great referrals either: they, too, will first try and translate, then implement the ideas you've presented from the stage before they realize they need you to come inspire, motivate, and teach their teams. Again, this leads to long, slow sales cycles without the top-down promotion required to secure the highest fees and increase demand rapidly.

EXECUTIVES: "HOW SHOULD WE" CONTENT

Above the managers on the pyramid are the executives. Generally speaking, the executive team is charged with putting together the plans, policies, strategies, and budgets for an organization. They also act in a supervisory role for the managers below them. When it comes to the content they value from a keynote speaker, they want "how should we" content.

Executives think strategically. They're looking for contextual models (which we'll talk about later in this chapter). They want frameworks in which to operate, new ideas, examples of others who've seen success—and they love industry-specific case studies.

Executives make very good, higher-quality referrals. Because executives in the audience are thinking strategically, understand the value of getting their team on the same page, and have budget control, they make decisions quickly and are eager to find ways to see their teams succeed.

Executives connect the dots between the ideas you're presenting and the impact it can make on their team.

There's only one kind of referral better than an executive: a C-suite executive.

C-SUITE EXECUTIVES: "HOW TO THINK" CONTENT

At the very top of the pyramid are the C-suite executives. These are the highest-ranking members of an organization, making company- or association-wide decisions on a day-to-day basis. These are the CEOs, CFOs, COOs, CMOs, and CIOs of the organization.

These executives want to hear big, innovative new ideas that buck the conventional wisdom. They're looking to be challenged and engaged. They love new thinking, new ideas, new perspectives, and, because they're at the top of the organizational food chain, they have immediate access to budget.

Win over the C-suite executives in the audience, and you've got your highest-quality referral.

It's important to remember that the smallest proportion of the audience generates the highest-quality, fastest-closing referral. Which is why the number of high-quality stageside leads you secure is directly proportional to the number of executives and C-level executives in the room.

Jay's referable speech is a "how to think" speech. It delivers content and advice for every tier on the Audience Hierarchy of Needs, including the C-level.

As you work down the Audience Hierarchy of Needs, the quality of the referral dilutes. If you're not fielding stageside leads from those top two tiers of the pyramid, you should consider reworking your speech. Still, a referable speaker doesn't pander to any single tier of the pyramid. A referable speech is designed to reach every tier on the Audience Hierarchy of Needs present in the room.

We recommend that you start using the audience feedback you receive in person at the event to evaluate the effectiveness of your referable speech.

Imagine you're at lunch with attendees after your morning keynote and you receive the following two comments about your session.

Comment One: "I loved your session! That was so helpful. My boss was in the audience; I hope she liked it as much as I did. I'll be sure to tell her how much I was learning. Do you do workshops or training for small groups?"

Comment Two: "Wow. That session really hit hard. It completely changed my thinking about how we approach our business. I'd love for the rest of my team to have the same mindshift. We have an all-hands meeting every May in Denver. Would you be able to do that same session for our small team of ninety people?"

These are both great comments. The feedback is positive. Both attendees loved your session. They loved your insights and both of them asked for you to speak. But listening for the nuances between them will teach you a lot about what tiers on the pyramid you're missing and which ones you've mastered.

The first comment is clearly lower on the Audience Hierarchy of Needs. While it's a referral, it's not likely to be a high-quality, fast-closing, high-fee opportunity. The second comment likely comes from someone further up on the pyramid. That inquiry sounds like a faster-closing, higher-fee gig.

You want more of the latter.

It may sound counterintuitive and even complicated, but the biggest names in the business hit all four tiers on the pyramid, whether they've done it strategically or not.

Most speakers find themselves focusing on the lowest tier on the pyramid, providing practical how-to content designed to deliver actionable insights to the loudest majority. (Which is exactly what event organizers ask you to do.)

Event organizers are looking for experts to fill their agendas. We know that. Meeting planners want subject matter experts, industry experts (remember Carol Walden's Industry Icons?). Event organizers must provide attendees with a well-rounded conference agenda designed specifically for every tier on the Audience Hierarchy of Needs.

Speakers who only address the bottom tier of the pyramid (the practitioners) fill breakout rooms, while the experts who challenge the C-suite—inspire the executives, demonstrate to the managers, and teach the practitioners—book the keynote slots. A referable speaker surprises the audience by challenging their conventional wisdom and hammers it home with some practical advice to make their insight feel approachable.

Remember Jay's feedback from his first breakout session at Content Marketing World? "Great tips & great energy." That speech is full of practical advice. It's packed with tips and tricks. It's exactly what an audience of practitioners wants. It's even what organizers say they want. Jay's content was useful, clear, concise, engaging. It's a good speech. Any meeting planner loves to see feedback like that. But that's not enough to earn the keynote slot.

Jay's second breakout session at CMWorld was not just designed to serve the practitioner. Instead, over the course of his forty-five-minute presentation, he hit every single tier on the Audience Hierarchy of Needs. He challenged conventional wisdom. He demonstrated how other executives have transformed their organizations. He taught managers how to introduce his ideas to their employees. And, yes, he gave them the tactics they need to get started tomorrow.

That's when his feedback sounded like this: "Great session! Would be an awesome keynote next year."

But addressing every tier on the pyramid isn't the only thing that explains Jay's rapid ascendance to the keynote stage. There's one more challenge he accepted, which we'll address shortly.

Jay Acunzo is an expert content marketer. He's spent years working for some of the most highly celebrated marketing brands in the world (companies like Google and HubSpot). Jay's bio is impressive.

Like Jay, you're an expert. We know that.

Maybe you're a marketing expert, a web design or a sales expert. Maybe you're a motivational expert, a fitness expert, a productivity master, or an HR innovator. Maybe you're an economist, a scientist, or an astronaut. There's no doubt that one of the major reasons you're being invited to speak at events is because you've demonstrated expert skill or knowledge in a particular field.

However, demonstrating your expertise to an event organizer, a meeting planner, and the audiences you serve is multidimensional.

The positioning problem

For the better part of a decade, Carla Johnson positioned herself as a marketing expert. And why not? As a prolific writer, Carla published nine books, consulted for some of the largest brands in the world, and served on the board of the marketing industry's most well-respected associations. With such a storied and prestigious background, it's no surprise to hear that she's also been invited to speak at some of the marketing world's biggest and most distinguished events.

Onstage, Carla is charismatic, confident, personable, funny, and engaging. Her sessions are always well attended, and she's often listed as one of the most influential marketing minds in the world. But for years, Carla struggled to earn high-paying keynote speeches.

Carla desperately wanted to make keynote speaking a bigger part of her business. As a marketing consultant, she spent most of her time working on massive client projects and a miniscule portion of her time speaking. Her revenue breakdown reflected the same: eighty percent of her revenue came from consulting and twenty percent came from her speaking. Carla resolved to invert those numbers.

So Carla worked on a speech. Beginning in 2015, Carla focused on delivering one reliable keynote speech at every single event. She crafted a signature bit. (A really funny one inspired by Jeff Foxworthy's "You Might Be a Redneck" jokes.)

Carla started conducting some empirical research to bolster her visionary hypothesis about creativity and teamwork. She crafted an onstage experience that included an interactive survey. Carla's speech got better, and she started earning more stageside leads.

It seemed as though her referable speech was working. While her demand was increasing, she couldn't seem to increase her fee as fast or as often as she expected. She couldn't capitalize on her compounding gigs.

On calls with prospective organizers, she'd emphasize her marketing expertise. She'd discuss her success with clients (highlighting any anecdotes she thought would increase her credibility). Carla worked hard on customizing small segments of her speech and even wrote custom session descriptions for every keynote opportunity that came her way. She'd listen to the industry's needs and demonstrate her understanding of their challenges. Her speaking was improving with each performance, but, unfortunately, she wasn't closing as many gigs as she'd planned.

Her plan to invert her revenue split between consulting and speaking seemed in jeopardy.

While Carla had changed her business model to more heavily rely on speaking instead of consulting, she hadn't changed the way she positioned herself to prospective event planners—and for good reason: she still needed the consulting to generate the bulk of her revenue. From the event organizers' perspective, Carla looked like a consultant who happens to speak instead of a speaker who happens to consult.

So, Carla inverted her positioning, starting with the fastest, simplest, easiest changes she could make. She changed her title on LinkedIn from CEO of Type A Communication (her consulting firm) to Keynote Speaker & CEO of Type A Communication. On Twitter, she added "Keynote Speaker" to her profile and amended her bio to include "World-renowned keynote speaker & author."

Over the next year, she repositioned everything from her website to her business cards to demonstrate that she's a professional speaker first and a consultant second. And, no, her consulting didn't suffer.

She stopped talking about consulting clients on speaking inquiry calls and crafted a process to help put event planners' minds at ease. Carla made sure that every event planner understood that speaking is her business and they could trust her to reliably deliver.

Suddenly, things changed. Event organizers stopped trying to convince Carla to speak for free (or for a lower fee) because the audience would be full of prospects for her consulting business. Event organizers stopped opening calls with "How often do you speak at industry events?" After she repositioned her online presence, she rarely, if ever, gets this telling question.

Today, as of the writing of this book, Carla has tripled her speaking fee and her revenue breakdown is inching closer and closer to her goal of eighty percent speaking and twenty percent consulting.

Carla is a professional speaker who happens to consult, and that simple change has transformed her speaking career.

The five types of expertise

Carla's positioning problem may appear to have been solved by simply updating her social profiles. But to truly realize the magnitude of her 180-degree switch from consultant to speaker, it's important to understand the five types of expertise event organizers and meeting planners value.

Not all of them are required, and, most importantly, the order in which you demonstrate the three most valuable areas of expertise to an event planner and an audience is crucial to your long-term speaking success and the referability of your speech.

1. ANECDOTAL EXPERTISE (I'VE DONE IT)

If you've experienced your topic firsthand, you have anecdotal expertise. It's your personal testimony.

You've lost the weight, improved your sleep, or successfully navigated a messy divorce. You've done it. You're the proof.

Maybe you've turned around a company as CEO or successfully executed social media marketing strategies for some of the most recognizable brands in the world.

Event organizers believe your perspective may be helpful, but unless you fit squarely into one of the Actors, Athletes, and Astronauts; A-List Alternate; or Industry Icon categories, relying too heavily on your anecdotal expertise is often not enough to earn you the keynote.

Think of it like this: As an event organizer you have a choice between the founder of Weight Watchers, who started her business after struggling with her own weight loss issues, or Bob, a man who decided to change his life by losing 240 pounds. Let's imagine that's the only information you know. Who would you want to put on the agenda?

If you said the founder of Weight Watchers, then you understand the anecdotal expertise dilemma: You're asking the event organizer to choose on the Fame Factor alone.

2. EMPIRICAL EXPERTISE (I STUDY IT)

When you've studied and observed your area of expertise, you've purposely set out to gather some empirical expertise and evidence.

Before Brené Brown had five number one *New York Times* bestsellers and one of the top five most-viewed TED Talks in the world, she spent years researching. Brené was (and still is) a research professor at the University of Houston, studying courage, vulnerability, shame, and empathy. Her two decades of recording and analyzing data give Brené credibility as a speaker.

But Brené blended her empirical expertise with entertaining and emotionally rich stories that connect deeply with her audience members. That's what made her a referable speaker.

Carla's newfound interest in innovation and creativity led her down the path of gathering some empirical evidence. She's spent the last three years trying to better understand how to encourage innovation. She's conducted original research to bolster her hypothesis about creativity and teamwork. She's even included an interactive survey in her speech to add credibility to her studies.

Like Brené, Carla can demonstrate her empirical expertise.

Event organizers love to hear that you have research to support your key insights, innovations, or revelations. But relying on your years (or decades) of observation and study is not enough on its own.

3. DOMAIN EXPERTISE (I DO IT)

Remember domain fame? Domain fame is not a measure of your expertise, it's a measure of the perception of your expertise. Domain expertise is the demonstration of your knowledge and skills in a specific sphere.

Jay Acunzo is a content marketing expert. He's just as capable and knowledgeable as Joe Pulizzi. They're both content marketing experts. They're both domain experts.

However, Joe Pulizzi is often referred to as the "Godfather of Content Marketing." He's written numerous books on the subject, built and sold the industry's leading content marketing website, and almost single-handedly popularized the concept of content marketing in the early 2000s.

So, while they're both content marketing experts, Joe Pulizzi has more domain fame than Jay.

It's likely that your primary area of focus or professional experience defines your domain expertise. Maybe you're a serial CEO and you speak about leadership, or a psychologist who talks about resilience.

Carla's clearly a domain expert. With nine marketing books under her belt (and a new one about innovation), very few people could deny her the credibility and credentials that come with a prolific publishing track record.

Event organizers are often looking for someone with a specific domain expertise. They might agree as an organization that their audience needs sales advice, or leadership insight, or innovation inspiration. Very often their need defines the domain expertise you, as a speaker, must help fill.

4. FRACTAL EXPERTISE (THEY DO IT)

Every meeting planner knows their audience is different. Tell them you speak frequently to business-to-business audiences, and they'll tell you that's great, but *their* audience is different. They're unique. They have unique challenges. They use different acronyms. They refer to their customers as guests or members, not clients or customers.

Fractal expertise is the demonstration of your familiarity and comprehension of those differences. The more an event planner feels you know and understand their industry, their jargon, their processes, their challenges, the more valuable you become to their event. In short, the more research you do into their fractal, the more successful you'll become.

Imagine you've been given the task of selecting the keynote speaker for the National Funeral Directors Association. You've whittled down your options to Jay Acunzo or Joe Pulizzi: both domain experts, both entertaining. Did you know that Joe Pulizzi grew up in a funeral home? His parents owned one, and he worked there for much of his adolescence.

No need to call Jay. Joe clearly understands your funeral director audience. Joe's a funeral director–fractal expert.

You don't need to have grown up in the business or even worked in it to gather some basic fractal expertise. Just an hour of research into a specific fractal online can set you up for success with meeting planners and executives.

Carla Johnson is an inquisitive person. She loves nothing more than to learn about an obscure business like ultraviolet light–curing glues. As much as she likes to learn about a specific fractal, it took her years to realize that she doesn't need anecdotal experience in every fractal to gain an organizer's confidence and trust.

How much do you know about balloon twisting, bathroom refitting, or running an HVAC business? From an event organizer's perspective, they want you to have some (even limited) fractal expertise. More importantly, they're thrilled when you demonstrate your fractal expertise on the phone and on the stage.

5. PROFESSIONAL SPEAKING EXPERTISE
(I AM A PROFESSIONAL SPEAKER)

Finally, professional speaking expertise is the knowledge and skill you bring to the positioning of your speaking and the process of working with an event organizer.

Do you present yourself and run your speaking business as a professional? If so, your professional speaking expertise isn't something you have to talk about. It's something you demonstrate. It's something event organizers see and feel.

Do you have a process? Do you return their phone calls and emails in a timely fashion? Does your contract look professional? Are you organized? Does your team know what they are doing?

Do you conduct an effective client "theme" call? Do you ask the right questions? Are you adept at interviewing company stakeholders before the event? Can you seamlessly adjust your speech on the fly if they ask you to cut ten minutes from your program? Do you know how to package your audio and visual files for the tech team, ensuring everything goes smoothly? Do you know what to do if the slides go down or your mic goes out? Do you have a process for doing Q&A at the event or know how to handle an encounter with a difficult audience member? Is speaking a side hustle or something you do professionally?

All of these things (and many more) weigh on the minds of every meeting planner. Hiring a speaker is serious business for every organizer. Do you treat it that way?

YOU MAY HAVE already connected the dots between the five types of expertise and Carla Johnson's transformation from a consultant who speaks to a speaker that consults. Before her 180-degree switch, every conversation with an organizer contained a hidden subtext: "I'm not really someone you can trust with your audience because speaking isn't my primary business."

Carla over-emphasized her domain expertise and under-emphasized her professional speaking expertise. Too often she tried to substitute anecdotal expertise for fractal expertise. On dozens of calls, she let her enthusiasm for her empirical expertise overshadow her focus on the organizer's desire for a fractal expert.

Carla's confusion about what an organizer values isn't unique. In fact, Carla faced one of the most common problems in the speaking business. Hidden in the subtext of Carla's conversations about her domain expertise is an implication that she's not a professional speaker.

Now that you know what the five areas of expertise are, you need to emphasize the ones meeting planners value the most. And it helps to understand why they do.

The Perception Pyramid

Remember when Carla first started to make the transition to being a speaker? She relied on her anecdotal client experience to sell her credibility to event planners. She touted her vast expertise helping B2B clients execute some of the most creative marketing campaigns in the world. Sure, they were impressed, but remember, they need a speaker first.

The Perception Pyramid

WHAT ORGANIZERS VALUE

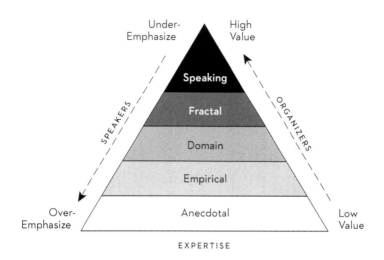

EXPERTISE

As soon as Carla inverted her entire positioning approach, things started to change.

Carla demonstrated her speaking expertise by creating a process for each and every speaking lead. She touted her domain expertise by showcasing her accolades in the industry but, on client calls, she'd focus on understanding the client's fractal instead of talking about her clients. Carla did less talking and more listening.

Today, Carla very rarely discusses her clients' projects (anecdotal expertise) or the research she's conducted (empirical expertise). Instead she shows event organizers that she's an easy to work with and reliable speaker running a speaking business, and that's worth paying top dollar for.

It's perfectly natural, especially when you're starting your speaking career, to have a deep-seated fear that
you're an impostor onstage. That you don't have the
"experience" the event organizer respects to put you in a
keynote slot. This might be why so many speakers default
to touting their experience in the trenches instead of their
experience on the stage when trying to sell their speeches
to organizers.

No matter the reason, you need to flip the conversation.

Showing your professional speaking expertise

Demonstrating your professional speaking expertise isn't
about what you do onstage at the event—that's your Entertainment Factor. Showing event organizers that you're
serious about the business of speaking and that it's a focus
for your business requires that you demonstrate what you
do before and after an event.

Don't *tell* them you're a professional speaker. *Show* them
how professional you are.

It's all about the little things.

For example, do you have an entire website dedicated
to your speaking, or is it a link buried on your "About Us"
page? When someone inquires about your speaking, do you
have a system and a process to handle each lead with the
care and concern an event organizer expects?

In 2015, *Meetings & Conventions* magazine released a
list of planners' favorite speakers to work with in the world.
In the top twenty-five of over a hundred speakers on that
list: Andrew Davis. Others on that list: Hillary Clinton,

President Bill Clinton, President George W. Bush, and Anderson Cooper.

Why do event organizers love working with Andrew? He's built a repeatable, documented process for running his speaking business, designed around the things that event organizers care about most. He's built a system that takes the emotion out of the decision-making process, and he's constantly adjusting the system to deliver an experience event organizers appreciate.

No matter what you do, your professional speaking career will only be improved by crafting an experience for each and every referral that's high-touch, personal, and responsive.

The key to building and maintaining a sustainable speaking business is to build a process that is designed to be event organizer–friendly. The easier you are to work with, the more gigs you'll book and the higher the fee you'll command. You'll also need a process for vetting, negotiating, closing, and then delivering a consistent experience for every event you serve.

No detail is too small. No step in the process you build should be skipped or missed.

You'll win more gigs, more often, when you craft a professional speaking experience that demonstrates your understanding of the event planner's needs. We guarantee it.

We told you there were two things Jay understood and embraced that rapidly earned him those executive-level stageside leads. The first is his keen comprehension of the Audience Hierarchy of Needs and his ability to appease every tier with the right kind of content. And the second is his elegant introduction of a contextual model in every speech he delivers. Jay Acunzo isn't the only one who uses a contextual model to craft a referable speech. Carla has one. So does Michael Brenner.

Contextual models

Michael Brenner has always put the customer first. In every single one of his fifty-three jobs (yes, fifty-three), he's worked hard to serve the customer's best interest. Often to his own detriment. As a salesperson for one of the largest software companies in the world, he put his customers' needs ahead of his company's profits, often recommending a competitor's product to prospects he believed would be better served. Michael's sales manager wasn't impressed.

Ironically, Michael Brenner's customer-first strategy turned him into one of the most successful software marketers in the business. His unwavering desire to answer every customer question and concern helped transform tiny start-ups into powerhouses.

Michael rose up the organizational ranks becoming a C-level executive at one of the fastest-growing software companies in the country. Soon he was invited to share his secrets of software marketing success at conferences and association events of all kinds.

Michael put together fun presentations, sharing his simple secret to success: put the customer first. In every presentation, he shared his anecdotal expertise of how he'd transformed organizations from profit first to customer first, often sharing the exact numbers he'd achieved.

He preached his idea with passion and humility. Sure, the sessions were well received. His anecdotal experience had led to significant domain fame that helped fill the rooms in which he spoke. But something was missing.

Michael Brenner's core message seemed trivial. It lacked weight, power, depth, and strategic insight. After each session, he'd hear from audience members who believed in the message but struggled to make the change in their own organization. Furthermore, Michael's speech failed to generate stageside leads, and he desperately wanted the corporate world to wake up and follow his lead: put the customer first!

Michael Brenner was frustrated.

"Why aren't my audiences embracing this change?" Michael asked Andrew Davis as they sat in front of a dry-erase board in a New York City office tower.

Over the next four hours, Michael filled that board with illustrations of the problem his audience faced and tried to map out the leap he needed his audience to make. He took snapshots of his ideas, wiped the board clean, and drew some more. He sketched squares and flowcharts, Venn diagrams and pie charts, magic quadrants and line charts. By the end of the day, he had drawn a new concept that he thought might help: the Bullseye Org Chart.

Michael had just created a new *contextual model*: a simplified description of a system or idea designed to clarify a complicated thought, suggestion, or course of action.

At his next speaking gig he debuted the new model, and everything began to change. Audiences loved it. Every time the contextual model came up in his keynote, audiences would whip out their phones and start taking pictures. He

The Bullseye Org Chart

© MICHAEL BRENNER

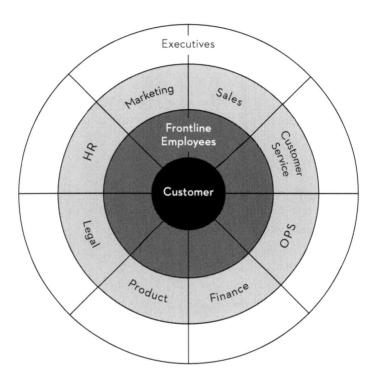

watched as the note takers up front drew his new model in their notebook. Images of his Bullseye Org Chart started showing up on social media.

Over the next year, The Bullseye Org Chart became the central solution that any organization could embrace to enact change. More importantly, executives started embracing the idea, and his stageside leads started to roll in.

Michael transformed his speech from a commodity experience about putting the customer first to a visionary keynote that challenged the way people saw the corporate world, and all it took was a smart, simple, and clearly articulated contextual model.

In 2019, Michael Brenner published his third book: *Mean People Suck: How Empathy Leads to Bigger Profits and a Better Life.* At the center of that book is The Bullseye Org Chart that he honed over dozens and dozens of keynote speeches to audiences around the world.

We know that there are a number of ways to demonstrate and share your domain expertise with an audience. Some speakers are magnificent storytellers. Others transform data into insights without slides full of charts and graphs. However, there's one thing that separates the visionary speakers from the commodity keynotes: a contextual model.

Jay Acunzo's signature speech culminates with the building of a contextual model designed to help organizations leap from following the best practices to trusting their intuition.

The Unthinkable

© JAY ACUNZO

The Perpetual Innovation Process

© CARLA JOHNSON

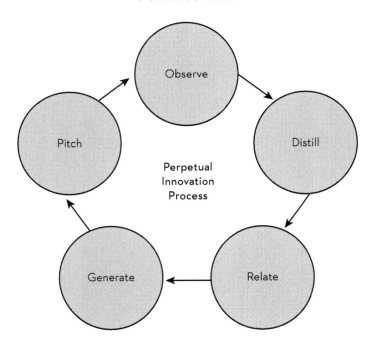

Carla Johnson uses a contextual model in her speech about innovation too: the Perpetual Innovation Process.

This contextual model is at the core of Carla's tenth book: *RE:Think Innovation: How the World's Most Prolific Innovators Come Up with Great Ideas That Turn into Extraordinary Outcomes.*

A contextual model shows that you've created your own proprietary processes or innovative way of seeing the world. It helps you demonstrate your signature intellectual property in an easy-to-understand way. More importantly, it shifts the way your audience sees the world. Without it, you're essentially presenting commodity concepts.

At the epicenter of Simon Sinek's bestselling book *Start with Why*, and his TED Talk "How Great Leaders Inspire Action," is the Golden Circle. It's a contextual model—a drawing that illustrates complex ideas. With concentric rings, like a target, Sinek's contextual model helps support his big idea: people don't buy *what* you do, they buy *why* you do it.

The Golden Circle

© SIMON SINEK

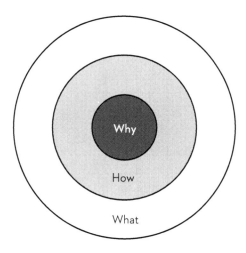

Inspired by an age-old mathematical formula called the golden ratio, Sinek's Golden Circle helps him teach people to start everything they do with first asking why. It made his content easy to consume while setting him and his thinking apart from other experts. A key component of his keynote, it made him a visionary, propelling him into a very successful speaking, consulting, and writing career.

Contextual models elevate a speaker's thinking and solidify their ideas. Contextual models differentiate your speech, and they're a crucial component of a referable speech. Most of the speakers we've profiled in this book have a contextual model as a key component in their speech.

Contextual models that work

An effective contextual model is more than a pie chart, a donut chart, or a standard-issue Venn diagram (although we do love a good Venn diagram). It's not a pithy quote set over a stock photo of two people walking on a trail in the forest.

Remember, a contextual model is a customized proprietary concept demonstrated visually. It should represent your big idea, demonstrate your intellectual property, and increase the credibility of your content while making it easier to understand.

A contextual model needs to be easy enough to draw on a napkin, but nuanced enough to invite questions.

Dan Roam literally illustrates how in his book *The Back of the Napkin: Solving Problems and Selling Ideas with Pictures*. He says that even people who believe they're not visual thinkers can learn how to create simple pictures that convey complex ideas.

We've used a number of contextual models in this book to provide context for you when we share new concepts. The Audience Hierarchy of Needs and the referral tree, for example.

Stephen Covey popularized the Time Management Matrix in his perennial bestseller *The 7 Habits of Highly Effective People.*

It's become one of the most recognized visual models in business, consisting of four quadrants: important, not important, urgent, and not urgent. Most people attribute the Time Management Matrix to Covey. But Covey himself found the inspiration for this way of thinking in a 1954 speech given by President Dwight D. Eisenhower. Covey's matrix better illustrated what President Eisenhower already explained. The only difference: the simplification of the idea into a clear and simple course of action.

The Time Management Matrix

© STEPHEN COVEY

	URGENT	NOT URGENT
IMPORTANT	Quadrant I **DO** Urgent and important	Quadrant II **PLAN** Not urgent but important
NOT IMPORTANT	Quadrant III **DELEGATE** Urgent but not important	Quadrant IV **ELIMINATE** Not urgent and not important

In *The One-Page Financial Plan*, Carl Richards uses a scale to show why it's important to weigh your financial capital against your human capital, so you understand the long-term consequences of your decisions.

The "One-Page Financial Plan" Scale
© CARL RICHARDS

A good contextual model uses an image to convey complex concepts with clarity. They must be simple, illustrate your concept quickly, yet beg a deeper conversation.

Contextual models help separate your thinking from the other experts in your domain, and, ultimately, that's one reason your speech is more referable.

Contextual models take time to refine. They take deep thought, consideration, research, and testing. Constructing a simple contextual model is deceptively hard. It's this act of simplifying a complicated idea that makes it effective. Michael Brenner's initial sketches took months to refine and explain. Jay Acunzo spent two years investigating the reasons we don't trust our intuition before he built his model. Carla Johnson has presented numerous versions of her Perpetual Innovation Process model (and she still feels like it could be improved).

Before you start sketching out your contextual models, there's one last thing you'll need to embrace and fully comprehend. It's the one thing we've noticed about the speakers with the most effective contextual models and the most referable speeches.

It requires no rehearsal, no marketing, no signature bit, and no fame. It's the one thing that accelerated the evolution of Michael Brenner, Jay Acunzo, and Carla Johnson from speaker to keynoter. It's the single most important change that Andrew Pickering and Pete Garland made when they decided to move from speaking for free to keynoting the world's largest social media conference.

It's the one thing that, ironically, demonstrates your expertise without your having to be an expert, and it's just a shift in your mindset. (And we'll show you how it works with a contextual model.)

CALLBACKS

- The biggest names in the business hit all four tiers on the Audience Hierarchy of Needs.

- Don't *tell* them you're a professional speaker. *Show* them how professional you are.

- Contextual models elevate a speaker's thinking and solidify their ideas.

- A contextual model needs to be easy enough to draw on a napkin, but nuanced enough to invite questions.

(7)

Out of Expertville and into Visionary Town

───────────

"ONE THING you can do…" says Mel Robbins in the last minute of her TEDx Talk. Suddenly she stops as she glances up at her slides and remembers what's next.

"OH! Oh, oh, oh! Wait. Okay, this is the last part. Sorry. One more thing you can use…" What Mel says next will turn her into one of the most sought-after keynote speakers in the world.

For the better part of fifteen years, Mel positioned herself as an expert. Armed with a law degree from Boston College, Mel weighed in as an expert CNN legal analyst. She hosted a self-help radio show dishing out advice on negotiating relationships. Mel's outgoing personality, spectacular on-camera presence, and experience as a licensed mediator landed her a weekly A&E reality show called *Monster*

In-Laws, where she helped families with in-law issues find a more useful way of interacting.

Mel was a professional expert with credentials and the broadcast media cred to back it all up. Experts deliver exactly what those practitioners desire: practical advice that's generally recognized or believed, what would be considered current best practices.

Not bad. But it's not enough to regularly earn the keynote stage. Meeting planners are not searching for more experts to hire because just delivering best practices doesn't speak to all levels of the Audience Hierarchy of Needs. So, who is able to speak to everyone—practitioners, managers, executives, and those in the C-suite? The visionary, that's who.

These days, Mel is seen as a visionary in the area of personal development and self-improvement. However, in our opinion, Mel wasn't seen as a visionary speaker until eighteen minutes and fifty-seven seconds into that TEDx speech in San Francisco.

"I call it the 5 Second Rule..." Mel says.

With her allotted time running out, Mel hurriedly explains how the 5 Second Rule works.

> Your mind can process a facial expression in thirty-three milliseconds. It can move pretty damn quick. The other thing that it does very quickly is if you have one of those little impulses that is pulling you, if you don't marry it with an action within five seconds, you pull the emergency brake and kill the idea. Kill it! If you have the impulse to get up and come dance while the band is playing, if you don't stand up in five seconds, you're going to

pull the emergency brake. If you have an impulse about, you were inspired by somebody's speech today, and you don't do something within five seconds—write a note, send yourself a text—anything physical to marry it with the idea, you will pull the emergency brake and kill the idea. Your problem isn't ideas. Your problem is you don't act on them.

In less than thirty seconds, Mel makes the leap from subject matter expert to visionary leader with the 5 Second Rule.

Visionaries actively form a new approach and question conventional wisdom.

Mel Robbins is a visionary. And she became one in an instant.

Today, Mel's TEDx speech is one of the most watched of all time. Translated into thirty-six languages, her book *The 5 Second Rule: Transform Your Life, Work, and Confidence with Everyday Courage* would become the fifth most-read book on Amazon in 2017... and the number one audiobook in the world.

Mel Robbins made the leap from giving how-to sessions to how-to-think presentations—from expert to visionary. It took Mel almost twenty years of experience, trial and error, speech after speech, to get to the 5 Second Rule, and she almost forgot to mention it. Mel happened on a referable speech and a brandable idea.

Jay Acunzo, by contrast, went from expert to visionary in six months. How is this possible? How can someone with far less speaking experience, less professional experience, and fewer accolades and accomplishments go from expert to visionary so quickly?

He's not a better speaker than Mel. He's not more talented than Mel. He's certainly not more credentialed.

The difference between Mel Robbins's two-decades-long journey and Jay Acunzo's six-month leap come down to one thing: Jay Acunzo set out to challenge the way we think. Mel happened on it.

We've mentioned, too many times to count, that your speech must transform the way the audience sees the world. A referable speaker reshapes our thinking, they challenge our worldview, and open our eyes to new ideas.

Mel Robbins transformed the way millions of people overcome procrastination with a simple, yet transformative tool. She broke down, then reconstructed our worldview. She challenged the way we think.

Jay Acunzo does the same thing. Jay's keynote has transformed the way tens of thousands of marketers view the "best practices" and the "tips and tricks." He challenges audiences to trust their intuition. Jay's keynote speech renews a sense of confidence in our own ideas. Jay challenges the way we think.

Jay and Mel don't deliver *how-to* speeches. They deliver *how-to-think* speeches.

Jay made the leap to a transformational idea more quickly than Mel because he intentionally set out to create a how-to-think speech. A speech that speaks to every level on the Audience Hierarchy of Needs.

Transformational how-to-think keynotes are highly referable. Typical how-to speeches are much less so.

It's helpful to think of this transition from how-to speech to how-to-think speech as a journey. A journey out of Expertville and into Visionary Town.

Picture Expertville for a moment. While it sounds like a quaint little town, the moment you arrive you realize it's massive. There are experts everywhere. Each expert sharing their tips and tricks. Just when you think six secrets to success is enough, someone pushes past you with seven. Around every corner, in every window, at every coffee shop is another expert. In Expertville, everyone is a commodity. No one is famous and everyone is frustrated. They work hard. They hustle. But they just can't seem to rise above the noise.

If Expertville is overcrowded, Visionary Town is not. It's a small, gated community, open only to those sharing original ideas and searching for new answers. Every resident visionary has plenty of space. They frolic in wide-open fields and write blog posts in quiet cafés where everyone knows their name. They're constantly asked to be a guest on television shows and podcasts. They have lunch with other visionary thinkers and dine on entrées of ideas.

Where would you rather spend your time?

You can wander aimlessly, like Mel did for twenty years, through Expertville until you happen on a transformative idea. Or you can map your way out of Expertville and into Visionary Town by crafting a transformative keynote.

Let us be clear: anyone can map their way out of Expertville. Jay Acunzo did it. And you can too.

THERE'S A formula for crafting a referable speech. We've laid out all the elements for becoming a referable speaker in this book. But there's one last challenge we invite you to accept: take the leap.

In order to make this leap from expert to visionary, you first need a tool to understand where you sit today and where you need to go. You need a map.

It may seem as though you too need to slog through twenty years of trial and error to happen on a visionary idea, but you don't. In fact, you can do it in one tenth of the time if you first understand how to spot the difference between expert sessions and visionary keynotes.

Expert sessions versus visionary keynotes

Like most things, if you know what to look for, spotting it is easy. The same is true for spotting a visionary keynote. All you need is a session description and a title. We invite you to pull up any conference agenda and work through our contextual model called the Visionary Quest Matrix.

We've pulled up the agenda for a one-day marketing and digital communications conference. But you can choose any event you'd like.

Here's how this works.

We're going to use the agenda's session descriptions and titles to separate the expert sessions from the visionary keynotes. We're going to find out who's in Expertville and who's in Visionary Town. The goal is to help you find the white space. We're looking for the blue ocean. We're going to help you plot your course into the Surprise and Delight category of the visionary keynote speakers. We're going to find your path to Visionary Town.

There are two axes we're plotting every session against. On the vertical axis, you're going to use the title and session description to determine what the objective of the presenter is. Are they trying to change the way the audience thinks? Or are they going to deliver practical tips and tricks? On the horizontal axis, you're going to determine whether the subject matter for the speech is something generally accepted and widely adopted, or if the speaker is challenging conventional wisdom.

The Visionary Quest Matrix

This may sound complicated. But it's not.

Most sessions will fall into the bottom left quadrant. Welcome to Expertville. It won't take you long to realize that Expertville is overpopulated. Everyone has five best practices or ten tips and tricks. There's no shortage of speakers and speeches to plot in Expertville.

On the top right, we have Visionary Town. These speakers and their sessions are most likely packed with new thinking. They're challenging the C-suite executives in the room to think. (If they're on the keynote stage, there's a good chance they hit every level of the Audience Hierarchy of Needs.)

Plot enough conference agendas, and you'll soon see a trend: the vast majority of sessions fall in Expertville, while the keynotes, plenary sessions, or general sessions (the big stage speeches) generally fall in Visionary Town.

Very few sessions will end up in the other two quadrants.

We refer to the top left and bottom right quadrants as *Obsolete* and *Confusing*, respectively. You'll find a session in the Obsolete quadrant if it's focused on a subject that's widely accepted and understood but it's positioned as a challenging idea. Chances are the audience doesn't need to hear it. The thinking is obsolete.

If you find yourself plotting a session in the bottom right quadrant, the speaker's most likely leaving the audience confused. Providing ten practical tips and tricks when they're challenging the conventional wisdom will have the audience asking themselves one big question. "Why would I implement those ideas? I don't get it." Chances are they've not bought into the speaker's way of thinking yet.

Now, plot your latest session description on the matrix. Where does it fit?

Chances are you're sitting squarely in Expertville, and why not? You are an expert. Maybe you're a marketing or sales expert. Or you're a fitness expert, a mental health expert, an innovation expert, an artificial intelligence expert, or a technology expert. Fantastic.

The problem is not that you are an expert; it's that we live in a world overpopulated by experts. There are millions of experts in every category. There are cuddling experts and plant experts, search engine optimization experts and educational nonprofit experts. There are even experts who help coach experts on how to coach experts.

Your expertise has been commoditized. And, just like any commoditized product, it's hard to get paid more by differentiating *your* expertise from everyone else's in Expertville.

It's your turn to thrive in Visionary Town.

But how do you get to Visionary Town, and what's the secret to getting there fast?

The One Question

The referable speaker lives in a very different world than the speaker who spends their time building their personal brand, their email list, or their social media presence.

Everything shifts.

Instead of looking at themselves as the product, they look at the experience they deliver as the product.

Instead of imagining their marketing efforts as the hard work, they know the speech is the work.

Instead of creating how-to blog posts and YouTube videos, they leverage the Audience Hierarchy of Needs to challenge those C-suite executives.

A referable speaker doesn't just measure their success by how much they charge or how often they speak, and certainly not by how much press they get. They measure how many high-quality stageside leads they generate from each and every gig. In person or online, it doesn't matter.

Instead of competing for the table stakes in Expertville, the referable speaker embarks on a journey to Visionary Town. Visionaries ask questions and seek answers. Visionaries form hypotheses and challenge conventional wisdom. Every single person we've profiled in this book along with the most sought-after speakers in the world have answered the One Question for themselves.

Jay Acunzo answered the One Question: why don't businesspeople trust their intuition?

Jay Baer: why don't business owners learn from their bad reviews?

Ann Handley: what would inspire marketers to take bigger risks?

Dr. Elliot Eisenberg: why is economics so boring?

Carla Harris: why doesn't mentoring work?

Marcus Sheridan: what is stopping business owners from sharing the answers to their customers' questions?

Anthony Jack: what could schools do differently to help the doubly disadvantaged thrive?

Clint Pulver: why do executives change the way they do business but not how they manage their teams?

Michael Brenner: where is the customer in the corporate org chart?

Carla Johnson: where do people get inspiration for their groundbreaking ideas?

Simon Sinek got annoyed that business leaders constantly start their marketing, sales, positioning, and messaging by asking questions like, "What do we sell?" and "What do we do?" So he decided to answer one simple question: why do business leaders start with *what*?

Mel Robbins got aggravated with people promising to take action without actually acting. So she asked herself: how can I get people to act immediately?

Andrew and Pete noticed their audience spent a ton of time on things that had no impact on their business, and they were incensed. They decided to answer one big question: where should I spend my time if I want to grow my business?

The leap out of Expertville doesn't start with a solution, it starts with one question. A big question.

One of Andrew Davis's most-referable speeches can be traced back to the moment he found himself so annoyed at one stat he heard at conference after conference: "The average human has an attention span shorter than a goldfish." The presenter went on to explain that the goldfish stat is evidence for keeping your content short. "How could this be?" Andrew wondered. These very same people can binge-watch two seasons of *Stranger Things* over a weekend. So, Andrew asked a big question: how does *Stranger Things* hold our attention for so long?

Experts sell solutions. Visionaries ask a question Google can't answer.

Asking questions is the catalyst that sends you on a journey to find the answers no one knew existed. The journey is what positions you as a visionary, not the answer. The questions you ask send you on a quest.

Instead of following a path laid out by someone else, a visionary sets off to uncover the hidden truths, the underlying reasons, or the new ideas.

You don't need more initials after your name. You don't need a book or another client. You don't need a YouTube series or a podcast. Instead, you need hone your big idea. Edit and re-edit your script, stage your speech, rehearse your delivery—all the while asking more questions.

The key to making the leap to Visionary Town isn't to rush into a branded solution; it's to investigate the problem.

So, start today: ask yourself a question Google can't answer.

Your quest begins now.

CALLBACKS

- Visionaries actively form a new approach and question conventional wisdom.

- Experts sell solutions. Visionaries ask a question Google can't answer.

(8)

You Have What It Takes

———————————

RIGHT NOW you might feel the urge to immediately begin work on crafting a signature bit. Or maybe you're excited to dive in and build a contextual model for your current session. Maybe you're intoxicated by the idea of crafting an onstage experience that positions you as a Surprise and Delight keynoter. None of these urges is wrong. They are the urges that prove you're hungry. You plot your own course.

We suggest you work your way backwards.

1 Start by identifying your One Question.
2 Embark on a journey to answer the question no other expert is asking.
3 Build and experiment with your contextual model.
4 Address every tier on the Audience Hierarchy of Needs.
5 Craft a signature bit.
6 Focus on reliable delivery.
7 Build up your fractal fame to increase your domain fame, which in turn will level up your worldly fame.

8 Leverage your stageside leads to build a referral tree that takes advantage of compounding gigs.

Before you know it, you'll have built a sustainable speaking business.

These ideas may now seem simple to understand, but we know they're not easy to execute. They take focus, professionalism, and dedication. It's a big responsibility to rise to the top of this industry, and nobody's entitled to it. Remember, you don't *get* keynotes. You *earn* them.

There are hundreds of ways you can make your speech better, and dozens of ways that you can make yourself more marketable. We've chosen to focus on the tools that will have the greatest impact on how an audience experiences your speech and on your referability—because referability is the hallmark of the *professional speaker*.

You no longer have to make choices about your speaking career based on arbitrary guesses or unsophisticated advice. We never promised it would be easy, but we can certainly promise that it'll be worth it.

You have what it takes to be a referable speaker.

Create history

Referable speakers have the power to change the world.

So many of us aspire to do something memorable. We want to influence others or change the course of history, even in a small way. We want to inspire change and leave a legacy.

It's admirable to want to make history.

But you do not make history. You create it.

The distinction here is important.

The act of making implies it's formed out of something that already exists. It's an iteration of things we've seen or experienced before. It's the sum of familiar parts. But when you *create* something, it's brought into existence out of nothing.

You can create magic; you cannot make magic.

But you must do the work. Not the tasks. The deep, transformational work. You must be honest and accurate in your self-assessment of where you are today and where you are going, where you need improvement, and what to focus on now.

You'll find yourself making tough choices—big choices. You must kill your darlings and listen to your audience.

It's best to forge your own path. The journey to becoming a successful speaker isn't the same for everyone. There is no map—but remember, you're creating art, not making it. This is not painting by numbers. Be happy for the success of others, and you'll relish in their camaraderie.

You'll stumble along the way; we all have. But you're better for it. Others will stumble around you, and when they do, remember that anyone can tear something down. It takes courage and character to create something new, and you've got those in spades. So help build them back up.

Becoming a referable speaker isn't easy, but you can do it. That means embracing the emotional challenges that come along with a quest of epic proportions. Embrace the conflict and the emotion. They'll fuel your creativity.

To make progress with any creative endeavor, you must stay tough. When you feel overwhelmed, take a deep breath.

When you bomb your session, focus on fixing it. Taking significant creative risks makes you vulnerable, and when you read stinging feedback, embrace it. Your tenacity will see you through.

Now, don't make a speech that changes the world. Create one.

———————————————————

One of the best ways to maintain your humility is to surround yourself with a few trusted speaker friends who can keep you grounded. Ones who can spot holes in your performance or the experience you provide and help you continuously improve.

Hopefully, you already followed our advice a few chapters ago and gifted a free copy of this book to a speaker friend. If you haven't done that yet, do it now.

Head to **TheReferableSpeaker.com/myspeakerbuddy**

Write a short personal message, and we'll send them an ebook.

Now's the time to formalize your partnership. Give them a call (yes, on the phone), and ask them to be your speaker buddy. Start your journey with a friend who'll keep you honest, humble, and true.

Conclusion
Stay Humble

"No fame required." That's what it says on the back cover of this book.

We've waited until the very end of this book to address one of the greatest ironies in the speaking business: fame is a by-product of your speaking success, not its source.

A referable speaker lets the speech do the work.

Remember, fame is "the state of being known or talked about by many people."

Craft a referable speech, deliver it, and they'll talk.

Executives will ask for your business card and seek out your advice.

Hone your signature bit, and they'll share it. Deliver it reliably, and the audience will applaud it.

Challenge every individual to change their perspective, embrace a new idea, inspire those attending to act, and many will do it.

Create an experience—not just for those sitting in the auditorium but for the events' organizers—and they'll embrace it.

The more people talk about you, the more famous you become. With every referral, your fame factor rises.

You're earning your fame, not manufacturing it.

But we must warn you. The accolades—the ten-star reviews and those glowing testimonials—have the power to destroy all you've built. Those eager fans waiting in line to talk to you, those LinkedIn messages, Instagram likes, and the dozens of emails that flood your inbox after a virtual event feel good and fill you with pride. They're the reward for a well-designed speech, a spectacular performance, and your visionary approach. But nothing will put an end to your referability faster than an oversized ego. No event planner wants to work with a pompous presenter (let alone refer them). Fellow speakers will stop recommending you to their clients. The tech crew aren't likely to bend over backwards to help ensure your deck runs smoothly if you treat them like servants. Audience members will caution others about your pretentious attitude and your inaccessibility.

Oh, they'll talk about you—but for all the wrong reasons.

The hallmark of a Surprise and Delight speaker is their humble attitude.

Referable speakers are students, never masters. They make time for others. They share their insight openly, and they're never too busy or too important to listen.

So we're here to caution you of what's to come.

As your referral tree grows and you become more well known, you're going to feel great. Your speaking business will be booming. Those referrals will roll in, and the recognition will pile on. You'll field podcast invitations and interview requests. You'll see yourself quoted in newspapers and profiled in magazines. Event websites will feature your face on their homepage, and the first time you run into a life-size cardboard cutout of yourself at an event, you'll do a double take.

But the moment you let any of this attention chip away at your humility is the moment you destroy everything you've built.

We've warned you. You are going to change the world.

Every time you deliver your message to an audience—whether in person or online—you are there in the service of your audience. Whether you're being paid handsomely or you're speaking for free, you've been honored with the privilege of inspiring change.

So, go change the world.

Just stay humble while you do it.

Your Humble Servants,

MICHAEL PORT   ANDREW DAVIS

Acknowledgments

LIKE A stage performance, a book is rarely, if ever, conceived of, written, edited, typeset, designed, printed, and distributed by only one or even two people. It's one of the things we love about the creative process. If we're confident in our ideas while also being open to new or different ones, we can do more together than we can alone. *The Referable Speaker* is a testament to this perspective; many people have brought their skills and voices to bear on the final product.

Compiling a list of the people who impacted this book and our speaking careers is a daunting and impossible task. We've learned so much about the business of being a professional from so many. The names of most of those people appear here in the acknowledgments. But we've also learned a lot about being a referable speaker from speakers we have never met. We learned by watching others onstage, listening to what fellow audience members said, and changing what we did as a result. So to all of you we've never met, thank you.

Thank you to the speakers in this book who shared their stories, not only the wins, but also the stumbles and struggles, and without shame. Their generosity supports readers by providing an accurate representation of our special industry. A special thanks to Jay Acunzo, Michael Brenner, Carla Johnson, Trish Witkowski, and Caroline Nuttall, who spent two years sharing their journey with Andrew on their way to becoming referable speakers. Your dedication, trust, and success are a true testament to your character.

Our early readers, including but not limited to David Meerman Scott, Drew Tarvin, Tammy Evans, Phil M. Jones, Jay Baer, Jay Acunzo, Laura Rubin, Eliot Wagonheim, and Dr. Robert Baker, deserve a tremendous amount of credit because they didn't pander to our egos, instead giving it to us straight and even sending us back to the drawing board now and then. Your thoughtful feedback, comments, and advice helped us produce a better book. A special thanks to Ann Handley for your constant insight and honest encouragement.

We've worked with large trade publishers in the past, but none surpass the extraordinary experience we had working with Page Two, a smaller hybrid publisher with an impressive, flawless process that's atypical for the publishing industry. We so appreciate your guidance, skill, and patience, Amanda, Jesse, and Caela.

We have deep gratitude and appreciation for Jen Singer (aka Machete Jen) who helped us edit and improve the book. She never tires of doing great work and is relentless in her commitment to professionalism.

Sienna Roman, the brand manager and creative director at Heroic Public Speaking, toiled tirelessly on the designs of the contextual models for this book. Lots of people have talent—and Sienna has tons of it—but not everyone has the level of character she exhibits every day. And, of course, Laura Rubin, Julianne Hitner, and Becca Nutt. None of this would be possible without your meaningful commitment to the HPS mission and the people we serve.

We'd like to extend a special thank-you to Ron Tite, who not only shared his stories in the book and his insights during the process but continues to be an invaluable collaborator and tremendous friend to both of us. Generally, all Canadians are genial, but Ron excels even at being nice.

Thank you to the Heroic Public Speaking students who do courageous work. After all, we can't ask them to make big choices if we don't keep aiming higher ourselves. Their willingness to give us their trust with their personal stories and their life's work is a courageous act that we don't take for granted.

To Ryan and Patrick Brescia, thank you for all your speaking sales, support, and process refinement that have made this book and speakers around the world more effective.

Finally, we'd like to thank our better halves. Amy Port and Elizabeth Davis are our partners in both life and business. From Michael to Amy: Nothing I do is worth doing without you, and nothing I've achieved would be as meaningful without you. HPS is a full representation of the foundation of our love for one another. Thank you, Amy, for my whole life. From Andrew to Elizabeth: Your encouragement, support, and smile are my fuel. Thank you for your patience.

About the Authors

MICHAEL PORT is the author of nine previous books, which have been translated into twenty-nine languages. A few of them have become perennial bestsellers and made it onto such lists as the *New York Times*, the *Wall Street Journal*, and *USA Today*. Some have won awards from 800-CEO-READ and Amazon.

After delivering thousands of paid speeches on the world's biggest stages, Michael and his wife, Amy, built Heroic Public Speaking HQ, a ten-thousand-square-foot performance training center, to develop and nurture the next generation of professional speakers along with CEOs and founders, bestselling authors, business owners, and people leading movements and advancing important causes.

Discover why Heroic Public Speaking consistently receives a Net Promoter Score of 100 at heroicpublic speaking.com/testimonials.

If you'd like more support along with free resources and access to referral-only special events, visit heroic publicspeaking.com.

If you'd like to contact Michael, don't hesitate. You can reach him at questions@heroicpublicspeaking.com.

ANDREW DAVIS is a bestselling author and internationally acclaimed keynote speaker. Before building and selling a thriving digital marketing agency, Andrew produced for NBC's *Today Show*, worked for the Jim Henson Company's Muppets in New York, and wrote for Charles Kuralt. He and his work have appeared in the *New York Times*, *Forbes*, and the *Wall Street Journal* and on NBC and the BBC. Andrew has crafted documentary films and award-winning content for tiny start-ups and Fortune 500 brands.

Recognized as one of the industry's "Jaw-Dropping Marketing Speakers," Andrew is a mainstay on global marketing influencer lists. Wherever he goes, Andrew Davis puts his infectious enthusiasm and magnetic speaking style to good use teaching business leaders how to grow their businesses, transform their cities, and leave their legacy.

Want to learn more about Andrew Davis and the speaker software he uses to manage his thriving business? Sign up for his weekly speaking insight designed to help professional speakers reach their full potential at Amplify Speaking.com/ReferableSpeaker.

If you'd like to reach out directly, feel free to email Andrew at adavis@monumentalshift.com.

Printed in Great Britain
by Amazon

34771274R00128